AUTHORS COVERED IN THIS VOLUME

Catherine Aird, creator of Inspector C.D. Sloan and his assistant, William Crosby

Earl Derr Biggers, creator of Charlie Chan

Charity Blackstock, who had no recurring characters in her mystery novels

Elizabeth Daly, whose detective Henry Gamadge was a specialist in rare books and documents

Patricia Moyes, whose detective Henry Tibbett was almost always assisted by his wife Emmy.

Managansett Press

Don D'Ammassa is the author of:

Horror
Blood Beast
Servant of Chaos*
Caverns of Chaos*
Wings over Manhattan
The Gargoyle
That Way Madness Lies*
Little Evils*
Passing Death*
Date with the Dark*
The Devil Is in the Details*
Living Things*
Shadows Over R'lyeh*

Science Fiction
Scarab*
Haven*
Narcissus*
Translation Station
The Sinking Island*
Alien & Otherwise*
Wormdance*
Sandcastles*
Carbon Copies*

Mysteries
Murder in Silverplate*
Dead of Winter*
Death at the Art Gallery*
Death on the Mountain*
Death on Black Island*
Death in Black and White*

Fantasy
The Kaleidoscope*
Elaborate Lies*
The Maltese Gargoyle*
Perilous Pursuits*
Multiplicity*

Nonfiction
The Encyclopedia of Science Fiction
The Encyclopedia of Fantasy and Horror
The Encyclopedia of Adventure Fiction
Masters of Detection Vol I*
Masters of Detection Vol II*
Masters of Detection Vol III*
Architects of Tomorrow Vol I*

*published by Managansett Press

MASTERS OF DETECTION VOLUME III

Don D'Ammassa

This book is a work of fiction. Names, places, and events are not based on real people or places. Any resemblance is purely coincidental.

Copyright ©2015 by Don D'Ammassa. All rights reserved. If you would like to use material from this book other than brief excerpts for review purposes, prior written permission must be received by contacting the author at dondammassa@cox.net.

Managansett Press First Edition 2015

MASTERS OF DETECTION VOLUME III

CONTENTS

Introduction	7
Catherine Aird	8
Patricia Moyes	42
Earl Derr Biggers	87
Elizabeth Daly	109
Charity Blackstock	136
Index of Titles	156

INTRODUCTION

The authors included in this volume of essays are a mixed lot. Earl Derr Biggers is best known for his Charlie Chan novels, which are early examples of the police procedural. His previous work in the genre consisted of standalone stories that were more properly suspense than detection. Patricia Moyes and Catherine Aird wrote more conventional police procedurals, featuring Henry Tibbett and his wife in the former case and Inspector C.D. Sloan in the latter. Elizabeth Daly's detective, Henry Gamadge, is a talented amateur in the tradition of John Dickson Carr and Dorothy L. Sayers. Charity Blackstock had no recurring characters at all. Each of her novels stands by itself and they are much more clearly suspense novels, though some detection is occasionally involved.

With the exception of Blackstock, who wrote a much larger body of work outside the genre, all of these writers worked primarily in the mystery field. With the exception of Biggers, none would likely be included in the first rank of mystery writers, although their work was consistently solid and as readable today as when they were first published. Only Aird is still living. Aird, Blackstock, and Moyes were English or Scottish. Biggers and Daly were Americans.

CATHERINE AIRD

Catherine Aird is the pseudonym of a Scottish mystery novelist named Kinn Hamilton McIntosh who made her debut with *A Religious Body* in 1966. Aird, who has written a good deal of non-fiction on various subjects, introduced Inspector C.D. (Christopher Dennis) Sloan and his assistant, William Crosby, in this novel and they are present in most of her subsequent fiction. They are subordinates of Superintendent Leeyes, who is irascible and prone to uttering aphorisms. The stories are set in Calleshire and usually around the town of Berebury. Sloan, his boss, and several other characters make a habit of quoting from poems, plays, and elsewhere in virtually every book.

A Religious Body (1966) opens with the disappearance of a nun from her convent and the discovery of a spot of blood on one of their texts. Inspector C.D. Sloan is a seasoned veteran of the Calleshire Constabulary but his new assistant, Detective-Constable William Crosby, is relatively new to detective work and is generally considered rather slow and imperceptive. The missing nun, Sister Anne, is found at the foot of the basement stairs with her head caved in, but Sloan notices immediately that there is no blood on the floor beneath her, suggesting that she died elsewhere and had stopped bleeding before being placed in her current position. Subsequent investigation leads to blood stains in a broom closet suggesting that she was hidden there until the opportunity arose to push her down the staircase. Her eye glasses, however, cannot be found at either location.

One of the other nuns found blood on her thumb that same morning but has no idea where she picked it up. Sloan and his crew determine that other than the nuns, a priest, and a rather surly handyman, no one should have had access to the convent. But there are four doors and thirty windows, and several of the local people would know at least something about the internal layout because services are performed in the chapel. One local family owned the building prior to its becoming a convent and would certainly be able to describe the floor plan. It is also revealed that Sister Anne was about to inherit a substantial sum of money which she had vowed to donate to the convent.

The police find the footprints of two people in the yard, possibly indicating that there were unauthorized visitors from the adjacent agricultural school. The head of the school is Marwin Ranby. The dead nun was originally named Cartwright. The mother has apparently disowned her but an older cousin named Harold Cartwright shows up at the convent the day after the murder, pleading urgent family business. An anonymous phone caller tells Sloan that there will be a bonfire at the school that evening and he arrives in time to rescue the figure of a nun which has been erected atop the pyre. He also spots Cartwright at the scene, but Cartwright denies having made the call. An interview with the dead woman's mother is unproductive; she asserts that there had been no contact between them during the thirty years since she became a nun.

The effigy at the bonfire was wearing a spare habit stolen from the convent, and the eye glasses that belonged to the late Sister Anne. The autopsy reveals that she died immediately after eating supper, which contradicts the witnesses who say she was present at services later in the day. This suggests that someone took her place, quite plausible given the anonymity provided by their habits and lifestyle. The three young men who stole the habit are identified. According to their story, only one of them went inside – through an unlocked back door that should have been locked – and found the habit hanging on a hook. He claims to have been inside for less than a minute. The habit was hidden in a cowshed until the time of the bonfire, and it was during this period that the glasses were added by persons unknown. Sloan does not believe they are telling the whole truth. A key to that door is in the possession of a local man who services the boilers, but Sloan believes the threesome bribed him to leave the door open.

The most likely motive for her murder is both obvious and murky. Having died before her mother, Sister Anne's half interest in the family business reverts to Harold Cartwright's father. This would enable the company to more easily become publicly traded and the advantage to Harold is apparent. Although this seems to make him the most likely suspect, the coincidence of his arrival seems too obvious. It is also improbable that he would be familiar with the internal layout of the convent, although it is possible that he visited there when it was still a private residence.

Sloan is interested to hear that one of the nuns decided to leave the convent three weeks earlier. He is looking into that when one of the three young men guilty of the intrusion is found strangled to death on the convent grounds. When he finally interviews the ex-nun, she mentions that she was on the grounds of the convent that very morning, a nostalgic visit, although she didn't speak to anyone. Although she has no apparent motive, she would have known the layout and the order of events inside the convent, could certainly have contrived to kill Sister Anne and dispose of the body.

Sloan believes that the murder weapon was a removable post from the stairway railing, and that the nun with blood on her hand probably touched it in the normal course of events. The conclusion is slightly rushed and Sloan receives information that is not shared with the reader, as a consequence of which he sets up a trap to force the killer – Ranby – to reveal himself. Sister Anne was not his target; he mistook her for another nun in the dark. There are some minor problems with the solution. It is never explained how Ranby would have known the routine inside the convent. His motive for killing the student is unconvincing. He was afraid that the young man had noticed that the habit was warm when he stole it. His motive is not revealed until the end, which would not be playing fair in a traditional detective story. There are also too few viable suspects and Ranby seems almost inevitably the killer.

Aird uses a very matter of fact style and unlike many mystery writers, she spares us most of the unproductive interviews which are usually designed to lull the reader with a plethora of detail while delivering the occasional clue or red herring. She also steps out of the narrative to provide foreshadowing, e.g, telling us that the bonfire at the agricultural school will prove relevant to the case and later mentioning that a proposed apology to the convent from the school will move the case forward. Sloan is portrayed as impatient and a trifle supercilious, while Crosby is rather tentative and sarcastic. Sloan has been married for fifteen years at this point, but Crosby is a bachelor.

Since this is a police procedural structurally, it is less important that the characters be sharply differentiated. The plot is more concerned with the process of discovery than with setting up a puzzle to challenge the reader. That format generally requires that all the information available to the detective is also known by the reader, so it is unnecessary to have a narrator filling the Dr. Watson role. The use of foreshadowing in this context is unusual but not unprecedented. For a debut novel, this was quite satisfying.

A Most Contagious Game (1967), which is a blend of the cozy with a procedural, opens with Thomas Harding ruefully regarding his forced retirement following a serious heart attack. It is very much in the tradition of Josephine Tey's *The Daughter of Time* in which a very old crime is solved in the present. This device was used again by Colin Dexter in *The Wench Is Dead* in 1989. Harding and his wife Dora have purchased a large country manor house that isn't designed entirely to his liking. While sitting there one day, he realizes that there is something wrong with the proportions of the room and the arrangement of the electrical outlets and concludes – after taking some measurements - there is a hidden room. With the aid of a local workman, he opens the room and finds a human skeleton.

The skeleton is of a boy in his teens, killed by a blow to the skull, who has been walled up for more than a century. The workman who does the demolition work to reveal his remains remembers that his grandfather swore him to secrecy about the anomaly in the house, but even the grandfather was probably not old enough to know anything directly about the boy. Inspector Sloan does not appear in this one; Inspector Bream is in charge, but it is Harding who is the prime investigator. The police are busy trying to solve a mystery involving the strangling death of a woman.

Harding is curious enough to look into the history of the house, which was owned by a succession of baronets in the Barbary family covering the time in question. He does further research and discovers that one of the baronets was succeeded by his brother, his son having died before the father. He tentatively concludes that the boy, Toby, is the skeleton. Toby's mother is also missing from the local graveyard. By examining newspaper records, Harding learns that the boy disappeared and was presumed drowned in 1815, but everything otherwise points to his being the skeleton in the secret room.

More details emerge about the contemporary murder. The victim was Mary Fenny and her husband Alan is missing and the prime suspect. No one who knows them believes that he did it because they were a pleasant and compatible couple, but they did quarrel on the day she died. The local villagers are almost certainly helping to conceal the fugitive from the police.

One evening Harding is disturbed by a sound in the house. Instead of a burglar, he finds only the family cat, but the cat had been put outside for the night and all of the doors and windows were locked from the inside. He also begins to detect an undercurrent within the local community. The Reverend Martindale delivers an unusual sermon about the need to obey civil law and their housekeeper, Gladys, misses church for the first time in memory. Later that day, the cat mysteriously re-enters the house a second time. Inspector Bream informs him that Allan Penny has been seen in the village and that he is convinced that some of the locals – possibly including the local constable – are protecting him.

The two mysteries unravel in parallel. The long dead boy was killed by his two uncles as part of a plan to arrange for one of them to inherit the estate. The other emigrated after being overcome with remorse and his descendant, after receiving a letter from Harding, comes to England to help turn up the last few clues. The murderer of Mary Penny is forced to confess – off stage – and in fact that entire plot was just an embellishment of the historical case.

The structure of Aird's second novel obviously varied considerably from that of the first. The characterizations are much deeper, the protagonist is not a policeman, one murder is historical and the other almost incidental. On the other hand, she uses several of the same devices including meticulous research, logical presentation of the evidence, foreshadowing, and little time spent attempting to paint a particular character as villain. The contemporary killer is also quite apparent since there are no other characters to diffuse suspicion. The result is a nicely worked out puzzle story, although with minimal suspense and obviously with no chance for the reader to correctly extrapolate from the clues in advance.

Henrietta Who? (1968) reverted to Sloan and Crosby. It opens with what appears to be the hit and run death of Grace Jenkins, a widow who lived alone, her grown daughter having moved away. The daughter, Henrietta, returns to identify the body and discovers that someone has broken into her mother's desk where she kept all of her papers. Even more puzzling is the discovery that the dead woman had never given birth, raising the question of who Henrietta really is. Henrietta seems to be romantically involved with Bill Thorpe, although it doesn't seem to be a particularly strong attachment.

Since the autopsy revealed that Jenkins had never given birth, and that Henrietta was not her daughter, the reader will naturally assume that the murder is connected to the pretense. The logical assumption is that the desk was where she kept records that would have explained that connection – possibly a birth certificate or record of a baptism – but there is nothing there when the police search it. They also determine that the dead woman was run over twice, suggesting murder.

Meanwhile Henrietta is desperate to figure out who she really is. The picture of her supposedly dead father is also called into doubt when the local Rector notices a disparity between the medals in the photograph and those locked in the desk. The police have also discovered that the dead woman was much older than she claimed. So at this point no one knows the identity of father, mother, or child, and the only potential suspect is Hibbs, the victim's landlord, who may have given the woman a very low rent agreement as part of an unspecified legal settlement. Sloan is also mildly suspicious of Thorpe because of his eagerness to marry Henrietta.

There is a convenient coincidence at this point. Henrietta and Thorpe are in another town searching for information about her real identity when she happens to see a man who is clearly the one in the photograph of her supposedly dead war hero father, although the man disappears before they can confront him. Sloan even comments that this is a remarkable coincidence, a device by which authors try to divert our attention from this authorial intrusion. This is followed by a lesser one. The police are unable to find anyone with the name Hocklington-Garwell, the dead woman's supposed one time employers, but when they speak to a retired military officer named Garwell, he orders them out of the house in a rage. In addition to its coincidental nature, it seems unlikely that the police would not have pursued this issue when they had so obviously struck a nerve. Hibbs' wife also seems to recognize the name, although she says nothing.

Sloan learns from Garwell's aide that his late wife had an affair with someone named Hocklington. He also tracks down Cyril Jenkins, the supposed father, but when he reaches the man's home he finds him dead. Although it is meant to look like suicide, it's obviously murder. Sloan then visits the college Henrietta has been attending and discovers that Hibbs has been anonymously supplementing her scholarship fund and that the school was aware that she was adopted. They also know that her real name is Mantrip. Hugo Mantrip, apparently suffering from shell shock, killed his wife and himself and the child was taken in by the nanny. That means that Henrietta is the heiress to a substantial fortune.

There is more marked tension between Sloan and Crosby this time and their characters are expanded slightly. Although the mysterious nature of Henrietta's upbringing is quite well designed, its resolution is less satisfactory, relying upon a series of coincidences rather than logical investigation to uncover key facts. The identity of the killer is obvious for most of the book – he reveals that he knows the dead woman's first name before the police tell him. This was so obvious that I briefly wondered if it was just an oversight by the author. There is also some withheld information. The lawyer, who is the killer, had a secretary whom we learn was killed by a hit and run driver a few weeks earlier. Nor is it ever explained how he concealed the inevitable damage to his car. A promising opening is compromised by too much contrivance.

The Stately Home Murder (1970) opens with a tour of a mansion now turned into a tourist attraction. While in the armoury a young boy opens the visor of a suit of armor and finds a dead body inside. The body is that of Osborne Meredith, librarian to the Earl who owns the home, who was currently engaged in writing a family history. Meredith lived with his sister in the nearby village. The Earl still lives in the house along with his son and daughter, a cousin, two aunts, and various servants. A nephew and his wife are visiting and a second is in the area. The Earl's wife mentions that Meredith claimed to have discovered evidence that the present Earl was not actually entitled to his position.

We are gradually introduced to members of the Earl's family. The two aunts are elderly and old fashioned and they did not like Meredith because he claimed to have found evidence of illegitimacy several generations earlier, which would have meant that the current Earl was not the legitimate heir. The unmarried nephew is apparently in and out of trouble and is thoroughly unpleasant.

Testimony pretty well establishes that the dead man disappeared shortly after four o'clock two days before the body was found. The

Earl's son has a bad cut on one hand which he asserts he acquired accidentally. Almost everyone seems to have known that the particular suit of armor in which the body was concealed was the easiest to assemble and disassemble, suggesting that it was one of the family who committed the crime. The medical examiner indicates that the victim was probably put into the armor well after rigor mortis had passed, so the body would have to have been concealed somewhere else during the interim.

The document room is in complete disarray, reinforcing the theory that Meredith's discovery was the reason he was killed. His sister also appears to have gone missing. Sloan finds a heel mark on one of the papers on the floor which was probably made by a woman's shoe. Sloan also notices a spot of blood in the library which suggest that Meredith was struck with a blunt object while in that room and then moved. Sloan's investigation is made even more uncomfortable when one of the aunt's insists that the family ghost has been active, which means that a death in the family is imminent, a subtle form of foreshadowing. Less subtle is the discussion by other members of the family which suggests that Meredith's body was concealed to gain time for the killer because of some other event which, presumably, has yet to occur.

Sloan is convinced that the Earl believes his wayward nephew is the killer, which would seem to rule out the Earl. His son's injury is confirmed as having happened accidentally and while Meredith was still alive, and it would probably have rendered him incapable of striking the death blow. The wayward nephew appears to have an alibi because he was seen arriving in town well after the murder took place, although this could have been rigged.

Sloan gets a break through another coincidence, unfortunately. Meredith happened to be in communication with an expert on genealogy, the same expert who had recently disproven his theory that the Earl was not the legitimate heir. That suggests that the dead man had found something else in the archives that was important enough to merit his death, although since he had not acknowledged his mistake to the family, it is still possible that he was killed unnecessarily. Meanwhile the wastrel nephew has disappeared and, predictably, is found dead following an exhaustive search of the house.

This was the most traditional of Aird's mystery novels to date. It is essentially a variation of the guest house party that usually involved an amateur detective. The motive is generally if not specifically known almost from the outset – that Meredith discovered something important and had to be silenced. It is not, however, all that it appears to be and the real motive is only suggested quite late in the story. There are also a couple of relatively clever clues that are easily missed. This is a good example of the traditional detective novel despite the police procedural overlay.

A Late Phoenix (1971) involves another cold case. Construction begins on the site of a bombed out building across the street from Dr. William Latimer, who has just taken up his first practice in the small town of Berebury. The workmen uncover the skeleton of a young pregnant woman, relatively undamaged, and the initial feeling is that she died when the house collapsed during the war, despite the relative lack of trauma to the bones. Inspector Sloan is assigned to the case.

The first quarter of the novel advances very slowly and without much forward progress. The body is old enough that the death could have happened during the war or shortly thereafter. Its position and lack of damage is mildly puzzling but not alarming. More significantly, none of the characters introduced to date except an elderly neighbor and the doctor's secretary have lived in the area long enough to become potential suspects in the reader's mind, let alone the police. The only interesting discovery involves a brief excavation by an archaeological team just before construction started. Their supervisor was not present but he had marked the area he wanted searched, and someone moved his markers before they started. Otherwise, they would have found the body themselves.

Sloan learns that the house formerly was owned by the Waite family. They are dead but have two surviving sons. Harold is married and living in the next town. Leslie was something of a playboy and has also moved away. The first brother tells them that Gilbert Hodge, who is developing the site, bought the property right after the war. This adds him to our list of suspects since it is quite possible that he hoped to bury an old sin, and he would have known about the archaeologists. Harold says that he is not aware of anyone having gone missing around that time, but Sloan is certain that he is lying.

The autopsy finds a bullet in the spine, which makes it a murder case. Meanwhile Dr. Latimer, who has just learned that his predecessor committed suicide, is knocked unconscious while walking past the bomb site late one night. Harold Waite has also disappeared. If the earlier doctor did in fact hang himself, he never explained why and the last patient he ever saw had been one of the developers. The police are unable to find anyone who went missing during the appropriate period who fits the description of the deceased.

Waite turns up dead at the bomb site; his body is discovered by Hodges. Sloan is convinced that the previous doctor was murdered in order to prevent him from identifying the body if it turned up, and the construction might well have done that very thing. This focuses attention on Hodges and the other two developers. Although this is a pretty good mystery, the identity of the dead woman is telegraphed when someone mentions the disappearance of the doctor's niece at just about the right time, and since this is never mentioned again until the climax, it was not likely to be a red herring. There is no way to definitely choose the guilty man from among the three suspects and in fact Sloan himself is not completely certain until one of them commits suicide rather than be interviewed again.

Aird's next novel was *His Burial Too* (1973). Fenella Tindall has returned from Italy to keep house for her father, but one morning she arises late and discovers that he is missing and that his bed has not been slept in. Richard Tindall was head of a research company in the area. His secretary is Hilda Holroyd and his second in command is Henry Pysden. One of the company project files – for United Mellemetrics – seems to have gone with Tindall. The night of his disappearance, Tindall had dined with George and Marcia Osborne and he had told them that he had to stop and see someone else on his way home, but didn't mention a name. Since we are privy to the daughter's thoughts for part of the novel, she is obviously not the villain. The missing man's car is in the garage, but the key has not been returned to its usual place, suggesting that someone else may have put it there, or that Tindall was interrupted as he was arriving.

Tindall, as it happens, had complained to the police on the day of his disappearance about a traffic tie-up caused by road maintenance. Aird provides plenty of foreshadowing that the traffic problems are important to the solution. A client of Tindall's firm, Gordon

Cranswick, turns up and is most insistent that he needs to speak to the missing man. He tells the daughter that her father had agreed on the previous day to sell his company to Cranswick. Sloan also learns that one of Tindall's employees, Paul Blake, was wooing his daughter but there is no indication that Fenella reciprocated.

Tindall's body turns up, crushed by fallen masonry inside a church tower that was undergoing renovation. A ladder has been moved from its normal storage place but it is not long enough to have reached to the roof. The hatchway there was in any case locked. If someone pushed the sculpture so that it fell on Tindall, that person would seemingly have to have remained inside the tower. Wedges are found in the wreckage and Sloan theorizes that it was propped up to fall when pushed somehow, probably by means of a window too small for a person to pass through. Tindall had already been knocked unconscious when he was crushed.

Fenella had spent the evening during which her father disappeared entertaining a visitor from Italy named Mardoni, who supposedly flew back home before eleven o'clock, but it turns out that he never boarded the plane. A man with a fishing rod was seen near the church tower during the crucial period by two neighbors. The missing confidential report was supposedly given to Tindall by Pysden that afternoon, although no one saw the exchange. It also appears that Tyndall had just picked up some very expensive jewelry, which he indicated was a birthday present, although he is not known to have had any female companions. The only female character who potentially fills that role is Marcia Osborne

This leaves us with several motives – concern over the sale of the company, a possible affair with a married woman, and the contents of the missing confidential report. The reader must also consider Blake's interest in marrying into the family and the possible similar ambitions of the missing Italian. The potential buyer, Cranswick, George Osborne, and the owner of the company whose file is missing, Wellow, have all dropped out of sight. Wellow is found murdered, sitting in his car. Marcia Osborne shows up wearing the mysterious jewelry, but she insists that it was a gift from her husband, arranged by Tindall so that she wouldn't find out in advance.

We learn a little more about Sloan this time around. He raises roses and enters them into competitions. This was also the first time

Aird made use of a locked room, the tower. The solution involves a fairly clever engineering principle, but the fact that only one character had a strong alibi for the time in question makes it too obvious that he is the one who had the opportunity as well as the strongest motive for making everyone believe that the killer struck at a time other than when he actually did. The crime itself is very cleverly devised but the identity of the killer is not as well concealed.

Slight Mourning (1975) opens at the funeral of William Fent, who died in an automobile accident. The police are interested because the autopsy shows that he had recently been administered what would have been a fatal dose of poison if he had lived long enough for it to take effect. Fent was just leaving a dinner party with eleven other people, who are naturally the cast of suspects. Inspector – now Superintendent – Bream from *A Most Contagious Game* has a cameo appearance at the funeral service but this is another case for C.D. Sloan.

We catch our first glimpse of each of the dinner guests through the eye of Cynthia Paterson, a local woman who watches as they enter the church for the funeral service. She also attended the dinner. Since the medical examiner had been reluctant to state that it was attempted murder and since he is unable initially to identify the poison specifically, the police are circumspect about their investigation. They don't want to blacken the characters of innocent people if it was not a malicious act, and they don't want to warn off the guilty party if their suspicions are correct.

The deceased was interested in developing some open land that he owned and had been trying to organize financing for the project at the time of his death. Although this is promising ground for a motive, Aird does little sorting out of the various characters during the first third of the story and in fact adds two new ones, the grocer who supplied the food and a neighbor who stopped by briefly but who was gone at the time the victim is presumed to have ingested the poison. A cousin named Quentin – who attended the dinner - seems to be a bit of a wastrel and is clearly experiencing financial difficulties. The widow faints when she learns that two detectives attended the funeral.

The dead man was only on the road at all because he was taking home a guest who was supposed to have been given a ride by a doctor and his wife, but they were called away by a message on their answering machine requesting medical help, an anonymous message that may have been bogus. The terms of the will are also suggestive. Although the widow is provided for, the property is entailed and thus passes to Quentin, although only if he survives for thirty days. If he does not, title passes to a distant relative who emigrated to Australia whom no one knows and down through his descendants, if any. This is particularly crucial because Quentin cannot sell the property without the permission of the next in line even after thirty days.

Sloan consults his wife who explains to him how the twelve people would have been arranged around the table given their social status. This means that the killer could have known in advance where people were likely to sit, and a cold soup had been dished out before the guests arrived, so it would be a simple matter to put the poison – a barbiturate – into the correct plate. And all of the guests had a legitimate reason for having access to barbiturates. The puzzle simplifies itself somewhat when Sloan learns that the cryptic message for the doctor was genuine and not part of the murder plot.

Although the missing uncle has died in Australia, he had a son, Peter Fent, which mean that the entail might possibly be broken if he can be located, which turns out to be difficult. Sloan adds the kitchen help to the list of potential suspects. One of the dinner guests – Renville – is involved in the project to develop the Fent land and may have been at odds with the victim. Another guest, Marjorie Marchmont, is found strangled in a park, and several of the suspects were in or near the area at the crucial time. Sloan also speculates that the poison was in the pudding and that the wrong person might have been killed. This is reinforced by the fact that the widow became frantic when she learned of Marchmont's murder and tried to flee the area.

The solution cheats mildly in that we don't know that William Fent was sterile until Sloan includes it in his summing up. That knowledge would have immediately suggested that his wife was pregnant and that this was the motive for the murder. This would also have identified the doctor from the group as the killer, since presumably he would have signed the death certificate indicating that the death was due to natural causes. The emergency call altered his plans. There is one red herring – the next door neighbor is the missing relative from Australia – that is somewhat clumsily done and which is introduced so late that it really doesn't contribute to the puzzle. This was also the first time that Aird made use of an extensive flashback, in this case to the night of the dinner party, to provide information and differentiate her characters. It's an interesting story with some minor structural problems. As a slight bonus, Sloan's wife announces that she is pregnant.

Parting Breath (1977) has an academic setting, an imaginary college. The opening chapters introduce us to several members of the faculty and a handful of students. The latter are planning a sit-in to protest the expulsion of another student, although for most of them it's a lark rather than a serious matter. Challoner and Moleyns have an angry argument on the subject. The latter believes that the situation is being artificially contrived and that Humber, the expelled student, deserved what he got. Challoner is hoping to use the protest as part of an intricate plot to sue the university.

Another student who is not participating is Ellison, a self avowed pacifist whose room is trashed just before the demonstration – a sit-in. All of his course work and research is missing and he calls the police, but is reluctant to tell them where he was when the break-in occurred. The demonstration starts and while it is underway, Moleyns is discovered dying in the courtyard. His last words are "twenty-six minutes." He had been on his way to see the campus chaplain with whom he had made an appointment when he was stabbed to death. Elsewhere another student finds Ellison's missing possessions sitting in plain view near a fountain, and Ellison was seen in the vicinity of the stabbing. Seemingly unrelated is the unauthorized entrance of unknown persons into one of the laboratories and the release of some white mice.

A search of the dead man's room suggests that someone had already been there. It also turns up what looks like a seed of grain, and it matches one that was found in Ellison's room following the theft there. Moleyns had also made an appointment with a history professor, but hadn't shown up. The medical examiner suspects that the stabbing was done by someone with training in that art, and circumstantial evidence suggests that it was Moleyns who stole Ellison's property. Then someone searches the home of Moleyns' aunt, where he has a room, and it seems evident that the searcher found what he or she was looking for in one of the books, because only half of the shelf is disturbed.

Thinking that the killer might want to silence the woman who heard Moleyns' last words, Sloan substitutes a police woman and sets up a trap. One of the policemen watching the building is assaulted by Ellison, who insists he reacted instinctively when he encountered someone in the darkness – a not very credible explanation – and refuses to say why he was in the area in the first place. Moleyns' passport is missing as well, and this leads Sloan to believe that he found something on his recent trip to Europe, during which it is possible that he traveled to more countries than he originally planned. Perhaps he discovered something important in one of them, then returned to England planning to reveal what had learned.

There is some foreshadowing near the end when the author tells us that someone else will die within the day. Various members of the faculty have disappeared for at least part of the crucial period and some are reluctant to account for their time. The librarian is found dead shortly thereafter, bludgeoned to death, and the assailant is seen running away but is unrecognizable in part because he was naked at the time.

There is some clever reasoning toward the end, although the nature of the murder weapon was obviously a sword all along. The reader has no chance to guess the killer logically because too much of the real story is masked until the end, The killer is a foreign undercover agent ordered to suppress Moleyns' discovery of a mass grave site. Twenty-six minutes was an attempt to provide the longitude and latitude of the discovery. There is one very well designed red herring. The killer arranged things somewhat elaborately to suggest that Moleyns had discovered an old letter of considerable value and had stolen it. The solution, however, comes from so far outside the focus of the plot that it is quite unsatisfying.

Crosby occasionally provides some light comic relief in the series, but one scene this time crosses the border into silliness. Two students wearing white clothing and fencing masks are seen at a distance and Crosby decides they are ghosts. This undercuts the seriousness of the plot rather than providing counterpoint. Aird shows some ambivalence about his character here and in later books. Although he is described as incompetent, he is an expert at finding fingerprints and other physical evidence, works undercover successfully, and occasionally makes useful suggestions. There is also a bit of a contradiction. The student committee directing the sit-in takes great pains to see that the only illegal activities are conducted by non-students, but then sends a group of six to physically kidnap a dean, which is a very serious crime.

This is a badly flawed novel unfortunately. The seed of grain found in both men's quarters tells Sloan that Moleyns was the thief. But we've just been told that there is a new strain of wheat being grown in the area, which would suggest that both men had been to the same location, but nothing is ever done to investigate this possibility. And it is entirely possible that they could have tracked the grain into the room individually or entertained a third party who did so.

We are never told how the foreign spy knew that Moleyns possessed dangerous knowledge. Ellison's assault on the police officer is not explained adequately. Moleyns stole the materials so that he could use them to write a paper that was due, but it would obviously be recognized as a plagiarism, particularly since the crime drew everyone's attention to the material, and it would not have been necessary to disrupt Ellison's room. The medical examiner concludes that the guilty party is a professional assassin based on a single sword thrust to the heart. These elements are all thrown together loosely and are neither individually nor collectively convincing.

Some Die Eloquent (1979) was Aird's longest novel to date. Beatrice Wansdyke, an unprepossessing teacher at a public school, dies unexpectedly but apparently as a result of her diabetes. The police discover almost by chance that she had a quarter million pounds in her bank account and certainly did not need to work, and they cannot account for how she came to have such a significant amount of money. She is survived by nephew George Wansdyke and niece Briony Petforth and her brother Nicholas. The family is surprised when the police request an autopsy and Bertram's wife Pauline is particularly disturbed. Briony, a nurse, is romantically involved with a doctor, Roger Elspin.

There are a couple of coincidences to move the plot along. Crosby happens to have talked to the dead woman when her dog disappeared a few days prior to her death. Sloan's wife is having a checkup at the hospital and overhears an assignation between Briony and Elspin. The will distributes the estate among the various relatives, with fully half of it going to Nicholas. George, the executor, appears to be unaware of how healthy the bank account was. The missing dog, its throat cut, is found by Crosby buried in the garden. Whoever let it out of the house and presumably killed it must have had a key because there is no evidence of a break-in.

Although the autopsy turned up nothing obvious, chemical tests reveal an interesting absence. The deceased had not taken insulin in several days, immediately suggesting that someone had replaced her medication with an ineffective substitute. Her last prescription was written not by her usual doctor, who had been away, but by Dr. McCavity who is prone to blackout drinking. Elspin explains that he and Briony had not gotten married yet because her aunt had insisted that she finish her training first. The aunt was also engaged in some private research at George Wansdyke's company, where he is partnered with a notorious conservationist.

Crosby is waiting in the hospital, hoping to find Nicholas who for some reason is running from the police, when he is knocked unconscious from behind. Meanwhile, the police determine that only the insulin bottle currently in use was replaced with water, which means it happened after the victim had opened it, and that the water was sterilized to prevent infection, which means that whoever did it had some medical training. Since there are three doctors and two nurses among the suspects, this is of limited help. By looking through her bank statements, Sloan determines that the money was deposited shortly before she died, and it appears that she didn't know it was there.

The solution this time was pretty clever although the criminal is quite obviously nephew George. Sloan figures it out when he realizes that the murder was meant to take longer but was accelerated, and that means something was going to occur sooner than originally expected. There is a little bit of suppressed evidence only revealed at the summing up, but it's relatively minor. This was a decided improvement over the previous book.

Passing Strange (1980) takes place initially at a horticultural show and fair. The local nurse, who was supposed to be telling fortunes to raise donations goes missing. The winner of the tomato competition is so obviously of inferior quality that it has caused a stir. There is mild but evident tension between the villagers and the owners of three large farms in the area. Aird introduces so many characters so quickly that none of them except the rector and his wife make much of an early impression. The show is held on the grounds of a manor whose owner has recently died and the villagers are somewhat apprehensive about what the heirs might do with the property. The only other noteworthy event during the course of the show is that a rental car was spotted in a no parking area, but disappeared before anyone noticed who was driving it.

Nurse Cooper is found dead, strangled, her body concealed under a tarpaulin, when the tents are being struck at the end of the day. Evidence suggests she was attacked inside the tent and dragged out to an area which would not be under observation. Sloan ascertains all of this and learns about the mysterious rental car very quickly and from available testimony is able to determine the approximate time of death even without a postmortem.

One of the attendees was Maurice Esdaile, a local property developer but the rental car is traced to a Richenda Mellows. The estate agent, Hebbinge, tells Sloan that two women are engaged in a legal battle over ownership of the property. The presumed heir would normally have been Richard Mellows, but he was killed by a poison dart in South America where he was conducting anthropological research. Richenda is his daughter. A distant cousin, Edith Wylly, is contesting the settlement by claiming that Richenda is an imposter.

Richenda tells Sloan that she had talked to Nurse Cooper, who knew her as a child and would positively identify her, ending the legal dispute. She faints when told that Cooper has been murdered. This means that Cooper was probably killed to prevent her from supporting Richenda's claim, or that Richenda killed her because Cooper knew she was an imposter. Her reaction to the news, however, seems genuine.

The work crew notices a coil of wire in the grass. They suspect it might be the murder weapon so they mark the spot, but they finish their work before fetching Sloan. When he arrives, the coil of wire is gone. This strongly suggests that Richenda is not the killer, since she was not in the vicinity. She, meanwhile, is refusing to talk but lets slip a cryptic remark about Esdaile being connected to the dead woman. Esdaile insists that they have never met, although a large development project is theoretically contingent upon her approval. The furtherance of that project does not, however, turn out to be dependent upon the settlement of the estate. Edith Wylly is not interested in changing the existing plans and Richenda would not have a say in the matter until she is twenty-five; the trustees have already agreed to the proposal. It does not escape Sloan's attention that the lawyer, Terlingham, who is executor of the estate, may have stolen funds, which would explain the delay in determining the proper heir.

The mystery of the incompetent judging of the tomatoes is cleared up. Someone moved the placards after the judge had made his decision and departed. A local teacher concludes that it was a schoolboy prank and determines which boys were responsible. Sloan meanwhile theorizes that whoever stole the reel of wire used to kill the nurse must have had some means of concealing the rather bulky object. These two facts are linked when the boys admit that someone saw them do it and that he agreed not to tell on them if they refrained from mentioning that they had seen him carrying the coil of wire. The solution is well handled and sensible although the motive – monkey business in the management of the estate that would have been exposed if the trustees had taken over – is not really evident until after the fact.

The next in the series was *Last Respects* (1982). A fisherman spots the body of a man floating in the ocean near shore and reports it to the local police. They recover the body, assuming that he is a drowning victim, but the medical examiner has a different opinion. The story continues to follow Boller, the fisherman, which suggests he has a further part to play. We are also introduced to Elizabeth Busby, whose aunt has just died following a long illness. She is living in the house with her widower uncle, Mundill, and is expecting the arrival of her parents, who have been working overseas. She is very depressed and anxious, and not just about the recent death. Rumor is that her impending marriage has been called off. She is also mildly puzzled because someone – presumably her uncle – has changed the picture hanging over his dead wife's bed. He tells her that he gave the missing painting to Peter Hinton, her ex-fiancé, at the latter's request.

The dead man – still unidentified – died of a fall onto a hard surface before he was put in the water. There is less damage to the body than might be expected given that he had been in the water for quite some time. He had a copper weight in his pocket. A dinghy is found floating in the same area a little later that day, but it has no markings to identify it, and two boys find the ship's bell of an 18th Century merchantman that was lured onto the rocks and sunk. A motive begins to emerge at this point because it appears that someone has located the wreck, which was carrying a very valuable cargo.

The divergent story lines begin to come together. Busby discovers that someone has broken into Munhill's boat house and stolen his boat. Sloan assumes that the body was kept in the boat house for some time before being taken out to sea. The ship's bell is traced to a farmer who is clearly being less than candid. Hinton, the elusive fiancé, has gone missing and it is a safe bet that he is the dead man. Then Boller is found bludgeoned to death in Munhill's garden shed. This is the final clue that indicates to Sloan what is going on.

Last Receipts (1982) is structured slightly differently than the previous few novels, all of which have large casts of characters introduced early on so that our suspicions have multiple targets. The first half of the book only involves three characters of note of whom at least one is clearly not the murderer. The historical shipwreck turns out to be a rather well done red herring, but even though the motive is reasonably well concealed, there are too many clues pointing at Munhill for his unmasking to be particularly surprising.

Harm's Way (1984) has a noteworthy opening. Two hikers are crossing the farm owned by George Mellot when a crow drops a human finger in their path. Mellot's brother is a successful businessman who has a part interest in the farm. The police launch a search of all of the other farms in the area, including one operated by Andrina Ritchie, whose husband deserted her recently, vanishing supposedly with a woman named Beverley. Len Hodge, who works for Mellot, was involved in a bar fight with an unknown man about the same time the husband vanished, so there are two possible identities for the missing corpse. Mellot's brother Tom recently survived an effort to take over his company, but he did so because the organizer of the buyout, Harberton, disappeared, and that establishes a third possibility.

The body – or more precisely the skeleton – is found on the roof of Mellot's barn. The head is missing and there is no clothing, which makes identification very difficult. Mellot, his wife, and Hodge all act oddly when the police ask about a forklift, which presumably was used to place the body on the roof. A neighboring farmer's wife has also been acting out of character, disappearing at times into a heavily wooded area nearby.

A hiker mentions having seen a single shoe in the woods near the farms, and shortly thereafter she is attacked and left in a coma. Mellot's brother and his family have dropped completely of sight. A search of the woods turns up evidence that a man has been living there for at least several weeks, but he is not there at the time of the search and there is nothing to identify him. Harberton is linked with various shady if not strictly illegal activities and a large amount of cash is unaccounted for.

This was a novel in which process was more significant than results. There is no chain of evidence which could lead the reader – or the police – to determine the murderer's identity through careful analysis. The solution has to be revealed through the ongoing process of the police investigation, which includes elements of luck. As is the case with the best police procedurals, the appeal is in the unraveling instead of the revelation.

A Dead Liberty (1987) opens in a courtroom. Lucy Durmast stands accused of having poisoned her presumed beau, Kenneth Carline, during their last meal together. The motive is believed to be unrequited love. The case is complicated by her refusal to speak or cooperate in any way, and by the unrelated assault on the detective who investigated the case and who is now a vegetable. Inspector Sloan is standing in for him even though he has had no direct involvement in the case. Her father is head of an architectural firm and is currently out of the country, so his second in command, Raymond Bolsover, is in charge. Durmast's best friend is Cecilia Allsworthy. We see enough of her thoughts to strike her from the list of suspects and she also believes that Durmast is innocent.

The background includes the opening of a controversial nuclear waste plant in the area. The dead man had some protest leaflets in his car when he died, but there is no evidence that he was sympathetic to their cause. He was, however, a friend of the Prince of Dlasa, who was opposed to the development project back in Africa which his father had authorized and which was being managed by Durmast's father.

The solution this time is somewhat telegraphed. Our attention is twice drawn to the fact that Carline had a bandage behind one ear.

On the second occasion we learn that it was applied by Bolsover. Since a crucial part of the case is that the victim did not eat anything after being served lunch by Durmast, this is obviously the means by which the poison was introduced into his system. The motive isn't entirely clear, but for the first murder it was reasonably obvious that Carline had spotted something that he shouldn't have at the construction project. The second murder – an au pair from France – is the result of a coincidence and the motive in this case is impossible to anticipate.

The Body Politic (1990) also involves international complications. Peter Corbishley is a Member of Parliament who finds himself troubled by an unknown heckler at an innocuous speaking engagement. Corbishley is scheduled to meet Alan Ottershaw, a constituent, immediately afterward and during the re-enactment of an historical battle. Ottershaw accidentally killed someone in a small sheikhdom and had fled the country rather than face an almost certain death sentence. If Ottershaw is not returned to face trial under local law, the sheikhdom will seize the considerable assets of the company for which he worked. The mineral involved is essentially for the British military. Aird hints that something is amiss right from the outset when the host of the affair, Bertram Rauly, picks an unidentified object up from the grass.

A few days later, Ottershaw is dead, presumably from a heart attack, but the crematorium finds an odd metal pellet among the ashes. Sloan also learns that an ambulance was called to the same site the day before he was stricken, clearly a fake call and possibly to determine how long it would take to arrive. Meanwhile company officials speculate that the original accident was actually a set up to embarrass the country, perhaps perpetrated by agents of a foreign power who wanted to undermine their exclusive rights to mine the rare mineral used in advanced weapons.

Rauly asks the committee in charge of the re-enactment if anyone found remains of a chicken during the cleanup, which provides a hint about whatever he himself found that day. No one reports anything like that, but a crossbow was left behind by parties unknown. A possible red herring is that Ottershaw had taken Rauly's place during the re-enactment and died theatrically in advance of his actual death, but this turns out to be a crucial clue. His widow, Hazel, seems to be genuinely distressed, although her mention that

Alan arrived home unannounced, much to her surprise, also leaves room for conjecture.

Sloan speculates that the pellet may have been substituted for a harmless one used in the re-enactment to simulate blood. When he questions people as to the particulars of that event, he learns that someone unidentified had followed Corbishley around the grounds, and a suspiciously loose stone almost fell on Corbishley's head. This resonates with the knowledge that he has also been receiving threatening letters with a medieval theme, and with Rauly's suggestion that he too has received a symbolic threat, a chicken bone under his chair. It also turns out that Ottershaw's boss, Morenci, secretly attended the re-enactment.

The solution this time is in one sense rather disappointing. Almost the entire plot is a red herring. The first murder was committed because of a love triangle that was only suggested faintly very early on and the second is simply designed to confuse the police. The accident in the sheikdom, the heckler, the chicken bone, the man costumed as death, the threats in the mail, and many of the other details are all irrelevant to the actual crime. Although this results in a considerably complex mystery, readers might feel somewhat cheated by cavalier manner in which so much of the story is dismissed.

A Going Concern (1993) is closer to the traditional British cozy. When elderly Mrs. Garamond dies, apparently of natural causes, the conditions of her will are somewhat strange. Her executor is a grand niece she hasn't seen in years, she has requested that her physician do a thorough examination of her body, and the police are specifically invited to attend her funeral. Sloan and the reader alike will suspect that she believed that someone might hasten her along in her final days. The dead woman's house was thoroughly searched by an intruder or intruders immediately following her death. Her will requests that the local vicar officiate at the funeral, and he agrees with some reluctance which he refuses to explain.

A possible motive begins to emerge. A woman named Jane Baskerville makes quiet inquiries about the family. The chemical company where Garamond worked during World War II indicates that it is interested in purchasing certain papers which may have been in Garamond's possession. The company may also be involved in an attempt at a hostile takeover. The niece learns that her aunt left part of her estate to an unknown woman of unknown address and wants her to locate the legatee. The only clues are her birth certificate and a snapshot of a memorial somewhere in France. The unknown woman was the aunt's illegitimate daughter, of whom she had lost track.

The medical examiner is unable to determine much from Garamond's remains – she was cremated – but cannot rule out the possibility that she was murdered. Garamond held a substantial interest in the chemical company, which might have affected the buyout attempt, but she was also involved in a secret project during the war. The niece arrives home one night to find her house ransacked and a young woman lying unconscious in the yard, struck from behind by the proverbial blunt object. The victim is Jane Baskervillle and transparently Garamond's grand-daughter. The killer could have been any of several business executives, who are pretty much interchangeable. Sloan figures it out through luck and instinct rather than logic. A fair but not outstanding mystery that includes Aird's first reference to DNA as a forensic aid.

Injury Time (1994) is a collection of short stories. These don't have enough space to develop multiple suspects so generally the reader will know who the murderer is. The stories most frequently deal with how the deed was done. "Steady As She Goes" is a very short Sloan story in which he figures out how a man poisoned his wife even though they both had the same drink because he chose a mixture where the poison would settle to the bottom, and he never emptied his own glass. "The Man Who Rowed for Shore" features a brief appearance by Horace Boller, relative of a man who dies in *Last Respects*, and an even briefer one by Sloan. A murderer planning to dispose of his wife's ashes at sea drops them overboard still in their container, and when they wash ashore they are analyzed for poison. This one is quite good although the end is rather perfunctory.

"A Fair Cop" is pretty minor. Sloan helps find an arcane excuse to arrest a man who the police believe was planning an assault. "Double Jeopardy" also involves Sloan but it's not a mystery, just an amusing story recounted to him. "Lord Peter's Touch" is a vignette about murder among a group of people playing a scene from Dorothy L. Sayers' *The Nine Tailors*. "Memory Corner" seems like science fiction at first. An academic claims that he committed murder to prevent a young scientist from revealing to the world that he had discovered a way to read minds, when actually he killed him to prevent revelation of a scandal. The character's account is so implausible that it makes Aird's story implausible as well.

"Slight of Hand" is the first story in the collection that doesn't mention Sloan and is the first in the Henry Tyler series. Tyler is a diplomat during the years just prior to World War II. A drug dealer is receiving messages in a restaurant by someone in the kitchen writing on his food. There is an interesting variation of poison delivered at a dinner party in "Cause and Effects", another Henry Tyler story, and there is a fairly obvious murder disguised as an accident in "The Hard Sell." "One Under the Eight" involves the order of presentation of wines at a wine tasting to communicate a secret code number.

In "Bare Essentials" a woman is locked in a steam room until she dies, but Sloan figures out how it was done. He proves that an apparent murder was suicide in "Home Is the Hunter." Henry Tyler shows up again in "Blue Upright." He solves a puzzle involving some stolen pearls. "Devilled Dip" is a minor piece about a petty criminal whose horoscope proves to be true. "The Misjudgement of Paris" is an amusing non-mystery about the side effects of a businessman's encounter with his daughter. "Her Indoors" is a puzzle that parallels events in *Hamlet* and turns out to be a school project.

After Effects (1996) opens with the death of Muriel Galloway in her hospital bed, ostensibly of heart trouble. She was one of the participants in the trials of a new drug. Her son, Gordon, insists that the police investigate even though her death was not unexpected. His charge of negligence is based on the fact that his mother's doctor was a relatively young non-white woman, but the police also received an anonymous phone call alleging that the drug trial was dangerous and might be responsible for her death. Meanwhile Dr. Meggie, who is in charge of the program, has disappeared without explanation.

Meggie turns up dead, apparently a suicide, near the farm where another of his experimental subjects has just died. Meggie, a widower, was romantically involved with a woman who insisted that Meggie's grown daughter, Bunty, move out before she would agree to marriage. Meggie, it appears, was called out on a fake emergency call. Someone also called the hospital to say he wouldn't be in, presumably also the killer. There is a possibly unrelated attempt to break into the pharmaceutical company that developed the new drug by people claiming to be animal rights activists.

The postmortem on Mrs. Galloway turns up nothing unusual, but her son is further outraged when someone paints graffiti on his house suggesting that he was collaborating in unsound medical experimentation. There is clear evidence that Meggie was murdered. Then another doctor collapses and dies at the hospital, apparently following a heart attack. The aftermath telegraphs the solution when still another doctor attests that the latest victim was reporting chest pains and when Sloan realizes that the anonymous calls believed to have been made by a woman could have been managed by a man with access to helium. There is actually a brief chase sequence, unusual in Aird's work, before he is apprehended.

As was the case with *The Body Politic*, almost everything in the plot is a red herring. The disturbed family life, the medical trials, and the animal rights incidents are all camouflage disguising the real motives. There is a secondary question – why were the managers at the pharmaceutical company so nervous - which is revealed to be a case of illegal testing on their part. This seems implausible since they would have needed to document their testing before releasing the drug anyway, and it is almost irrelevant to the rest of the story in any case. Sloan solves this one by means of some genuine deduction.

Stiff News (1998) opens with a funeral, which Sloan is compelled to interrupt. Gertrude Powell, thrice married, now living in a nursing home, has died of apparent natural causes. The nursing home, a manor house, is associated with a particular military unit and their dependents, so most of the residents know one another. Her son receives a letter from her on the day of the funeral in which she says that someone is trying to kill her, which is sufficient reason for the police to order a postmortem. Aird then introduces us to various residents and staff at the manor and provides some of the dead woman's history. She was married three times but the second husband and his fate are something of a mystery. Special mention is made of Maisie Carruthers, a recent arrival. The reader also learns that the letter was written two weeks before her death and left with one of the staff members to mail after she died.

The medical examiner mentions that there was another recent death at the manor which was questioned by the attending physician, but that the autopsy had turned up nothing untoward. One of the staff members tells Sloan that someone searched Powell's room shortly after her death. Her son and his wife are looking for information about the second marriage because this will affect the distribution of her estate.

Another resident is a former military judge and he is of interest because of his reaction when his tattered greatcoat was repaired for his birthday. Something about that frightened him, suggesting that he may have concealed something inside it. There are some minor complications toward the end but it's actually something of an anti-climax. There was no murder at all, technically, but some of the residents were hastening the departure of those of their friends who desired it. The end is mildly disappointing but the variation from the conventional ending was welcome. Aird did not vary far from standard mystery formulas but she did test the limits at times.

Little Knell (2000) has an amusing opening. Colonel Caversham has died and bequeathed to a museum his collection of artifacts from around the world, including a sealed mummy case. The local coroner intervenes when it is moved on the basis that dead bodies cannot be relocated without his written permission and he orders the police to enforce his desire that it be examined by a competent doctor. We are not told until later that he is reacting to a cryptic anonymous letter sent to his office. Elsewhere, a man is dying of AIDS and is mourned, somewhat, by two sisters who run an animal shelter that is partially supported by an official of the museum.

Few readers will be surprised to discover that the sarcophagus contains not a mummy but a relatively fresh corpse. The body is of a young woman and it is only about a week old. Cause of death was a fractured skull. She is identified as Jill Carter, who worked for an accounting firm and who never came home after an evening at a bar where she reportedly had an argument with her live-in boyfriend. There is as well an underlying concern about a recently intercepted shipment of drugs which is likely to have repercussions among users and suppliers.

It begins to appear that the drugs are the motive force behind most of what is going on. The man who died of AIDS came into a large parcel of money shortly before his death, origin unknown. He consulted the same law firm where Jill Carter and one of the directors of the museum work. An unknown woman has a conversation with Sloan's wife after which a very expensive package of rose plants arrived, apparently the first portion of a bribe. The fact that the coroner was tipped off about the body by an anonymous letter, suggests that it was meant to be found at a specific time.

The interrelationships of the various characters are particularly complex in this one, providing a very intriguing puzzle with multiple motives and strategies to evaluate. The second murder ties in even more separate elements when the moving company's ex-employee, who is believed to have drug connections, is found under a pile of hay at the animal shelter. This is the first of Aird's novels which suggests that Sloan himself may be in physical danger. The end is slightly rushed but the explanation is completely satisfactory.

Amendment of Life (2002) starts off quickly with two apparently unrelated oddities. First, a dead body is spotted inside a maze at a private estate whose grounds are open to the public. Second, someone has been leaving dead animals and hex signs on the doorsteps of prominent church officials. There is also a kidnapped goat left abandoned near a church. As with the previous book, this one has an intricate series of connections among the various characters. Various people from earlier books also make an appearance.

The dead body is the wife of one of the partners in the firm that is putting in security lights for the church officials. She was supposed to have been staying the night at the hospital with her young son, who is recovering from cancer. The man who oversees maintenance at the maze, Prosser, is also noticeably shaken by events despite being an experienced military man. The owner of the maze, Mrs. Pedlinge, is confined to a wheelchair. Her nephew and presumed heir, Bevis, is on the verge of a messy divorce and is a neighbor of Prosser, whom he helped to secure his present job. Prosser also clearly recognizes the dead woman, although he pretends otherwise.

It is fairly clear early on that Prosser was romantically involved with the victim and he eventually admits this is the case, but he believes that her husband was unaware of the fact. This points directly at the husband, who turns out to be the guilty party. His alibi was manufactured by means of a hologram, which is a mild stretch of plausibility but not a serious one.

Chapter and Hearse (2004) was Aird's second collection of short stories. In "A Change of Heart" Sloan figures out who changed a patient's hospital records to indicate Do Not Resuscitate. "Due Diligence" features a henpecked husband thwarting his wife's plan to murder him. "Time, Gentlemen, Please" explains Sloan's solution to a problem involving the meeting place of two foreign agents. "Cold Comfort" is a locked room mystery set in 16th Century Scotland but the solution is a familiar one. The protagonist would reappear in several further stories.

The title story has Sloan figuring out the solution to a 13th Century murder. "The Widow's Might" is a minor piece about an attempt to reconstruct what really happened at a crucial military engagement. "Handsel Monday" involves the same investigator as in "Cold Comfort," this time solving a more interesting mystery. In "Preyed in Aid" Sloan's superior finds himself trapped into participating in a public debate with a known criminal whose guilt needs to be proved so that the event will not take place. "A Different Cast of Mind" is a non-mystery vignette. Food poisoning helps identify a thief in "Examination Results" and "Child's Play" is a puzzle about finding the key to a cipher.

Sloan solves a murder disguised as food poisoning in the rather nice "Like to Die." The 13th Century series continues in "Dead Letters." There's a dinner party murder during World War II in "Gold, Frankincense and Murder," the best story in the collection. A missing person's investigation takes a surprising turn in "The Trouble and Strife." "Losing the Plot" is an amusing non-mystery about neighbors with rival plots of trees. "A Soldier of the Queen" is similar, in this case describing a soldier's preparation for a day of battle, but the enemy turns out to be tourists.

A cat scratche's its owner's murderer in "Touch Not the Cat" and the ensuing infection allows the police to identify him. "Exit Strategy" is a method by which a woman with Alzheimer's is abandoned and placed in a care facility, but it doesn't seem likely that it would work as described. "The Wild Card" involves an innovative extortion scheme. There is an international problem in "Coupe de Grace" and Crosby finally handles a case by himself, a dispute over a garden, in "Dummy Run." Many of the stories feature characters from the novels, most commonly Sloan.

Hole in One (2005), as the title suggests, involves a golf course where a dead body is found buried in a bunker. The reader is introduced to a few members of the club and a few of the caddies, and learns that there are rumors of cheating in some of the arranged contests. Sloan has to look particularly good this time because it is the golf club his boss belongs to. There are so many characters this time that it is futile to try to keep them straight until the story begins to filter out the inconsequential ones, which is not always the best strategy to keep readers invested in a mystery. There are also subplots about a daughter of one of the members who wants to be a caddy and the controversy about the conversion of some of the property to a driving range open to the general public.

The body isn't identified until halfway through the book, which is unusual, but most readers will have anticipated that it is Matt Steele, a former caddy who has supposedly gone to the continent on a trip and who is romantically involved with the would be female caddy, Hillary Trumper, whose family were not thrilled by their relationship. A second murder seems like a logical outcome. The victim is a man who sneaked onto the course at night to pick up lost balls, and it is quite possible that he saw the body being buried or someone out on the course who had no reason to be there.

This was the first of Aird's novels in which the killer is briefly the viewpoint character, although he is not identified so the reader doesn't know who he is when he picks up Hillary Trumper, only that he means her ill. Steele apparently heard something while caddying that could prove damaging to someone interested in the contract for the construction work at the golf club. There is a chase and confrontation at the end, but all of the action takes place off stage. Aird never seemed comfortable writing scenes of physical conflict, which is interesting because she originally attempted – unsuccessfully – to write and sell thrillers. Sloan figures out the solution in time to prevent a third death.

Losing Ground (2008) begins with the theft of an obscure painting from a museum, the only point of apparent interest being that it provides the only surviving view of a local manor house before it was extensively renovated. The house in question is coveted by a wealthy rock star, despite its poor state of preservation. The land it sits on, however, is the subject of a proposed and potentially profitable development scheme. Someone has also started a fire in the new wing of the house and the firemen find bones among the debris, which attracts the contention of the police. There was also an earlier financing scandal which the bank covered up and a rabid preservation society that opposes the development. This all provides the reader with a large cast of characters.

The fire was deliberate set to cause little damage, but in the ruins the police find a pile of animal bones on top of a bunch of lobster shells, an odd combination indeed. Lobsters, however, are part of the crest of the Filigree family, who once owned the property but who cannot immediately be found, and mention of the shells visibly disturbs an official of the development company. There is also a hostile takeover of that company in the works. Sloan discovers that someone else has been looking for the current head of the Filigree family, whom Aird hints has been kidnapped – a nice red herring - and held incommunicado by someone at the company working in consort with one of the conservationists.

This was an unusual novel for Aird in part because there is no murder, although one is attempted right at the end. It is not, however, as tightly plotted as most of the earlier novels and several bits of information are repeated multiple times and to no purpose. There is no clear evidence about who the killer might be from among the four executives so there is no way of anticipating it. One might also be skeptical that a development company would not have had a preliminary survey done to determine that the land upon which they were planning to build actually belonged to them.

Past Tense (2010) rearranges some old themes. Jennifer Short died in a nursing home where she had resided without contacting some distant relatives who lived in the area but had never met her. She does, however, list them as her next of kin and since her grand nephew is out of touch in the Amazon, his wife, Janet Wakefield, reluctantly handles the funeral arrangements. But a young man shows up claiming to be her grandson, and the nursing home is disturbed to discover someone has been in her private room and smashed a vase which she cherished.

Her grandson, Joe Short, hopes to track down his grandfather, about whom no one seems to know anything. He also learns that the dead woman received part of the dispersal of a trust, but only after a legal battle with the rest of her family. For some reason she has specified that she buried in a small village to which she has no connection.

Meanwhile, Sloan is investigating the death of a young nurse, found drowned in a nearby river. The nurse had attended the funeral although there is no evidence that she knew the deceased. Bill Wakefield has by now returned to England, but he is clearly lying about his activities on the night when the nurse was strangled and thrown into the river. He is also next in line for the estate if Joe Short should die, and the more we see if him, the more we dislike him. There is also clear proof that he lied about his whereabouts on the night when the nurse was being killed.

Next someone digs up Josephine's coffin and steals the jewelry she was buried wearing. Joe Short tells the police that his passport has been stolen, which delays his plans to return to his job in the Mideast. There is evidence that the nurse's room had been searched and that someone also broke into the mortuary.

There is some excellent misdirection in this one. The revelation that Joe Short is an imposter is very surprising given how well documented his identity was, but once revealed a number of earlier events apparently of no consequence turn out to be significant. The addition of a local thug trying to steal the jewelry confuses things even further. The nurse's connection is the result of a considerable coincidence, but that's not uncommon in mystery novels.

Dead Heading (2013) starts with sabotage at a large florist company. Someone broke in and left two greenhouse doors open through the night of a frost, killing a large number of orchids and other plants, some of which were specially grown for a landscape gardener. Sloan is still on the premises when the police receive a complaint about a similar bit of sabotage at one of their smaller competitors. One of the major customers was Enid Osgathorp, an elderly woman who did not return from her vacation on schedule and who has been reported as a missing person. The owner of the smaller greenhouse is divorced from Norman Potts who is the estranged stepson of Jack Haines, who owns the larger.

The missing woman never showed up where she had booked a room for her vacation and her house has been entered twice, one by break-in and once with a key. One of the major floral customers who is in some financial difficulty following the death of his father has been acting strangely and another of Haines' competitors is clearly not at all pleased to see the police. He also has been doing a great deal of digging, ostensibly for the garden. He had a visit from Osgathorp the day before she disappeared.

Still another customer has a mysterious and longstanding grudge against Osgathorp that dates from when she was secretary to a local doctor. There is also a clergyman whose wife recently died. She had been saving to finance her daughter's wedding and the money mysteriously disappeared. She left a suicide note with a vague reference to the past. At this point the clues point to Osgathorp as a blackmailer.

Norman Potts is found dead in his apartment, and it looks like he hanged himself. But then the killer slips up and mentions something he shouldn't have known. The solution is rather obvious after the fact, which is an indicator of clever plotting and a story that doesn't treat the reader unfairly. This was one of Aird's best novels.

Aird's most recent book is another collection, *Last Writes* (2014), and the title suggests that she has decided to retire from writing. A great many of these involve Henry Tyler, a Foreign Service officer during World War II. "Left, Right, Attention" is a World War II puzzle story in which the protagonist has to decipher a coded message. "The Hard Lesson" is a non-mystery about an unconventional approach to teaching students the value of relationships. In "Care Plan" Sloan figures out that an apparent death threat is simply a reference to a line from Shakespeare.

"Sleeping Dogs, Lying" is an amusing tale about a woman who murders her talkative husband, and gets away with it. "Quick on the Draw" is another non-mystery in which the reader is led to believe that one of the characters is afraid of an imminent parachute jump, when in fact it's just a visit to the dentist. "1666 and All That" is another code solving puzzle. A man confesses to murder believing that he has been overheard in "Going Quietly", but the witness is deaf.

"La Plume de Ma Tante" and "The Hen Party" are both additions to Aird's series of historical mysteries set in Scotland. "The Language of Flowers" is a very good mystery in which the protagonist engages in a conversation and through logic determines who committed a murder. "Plane Fare" involves a man's ability to read upside down and what he learns by doing so.

"Deaf Man Talking" is a mild story of World War II espionage. Sloan solves a problem involving reticent suspects in "Benchmark." A cheater at cards is exposed in "The Queen of Hearts" and Sloan identifies a poisoner in the very good "In the Family Way." Tyler solves a thorny diplomatic problem in "These for Remembrance."

"Stars in Their Courses" is a non-mystery about some troublesome guests in a posh restaurant, and "A Managed Retreat" involves shenanigans attendant upon the sale of a house. "Spite and Malice" is another historical Scottish mystery. "Business Plan" is an amusing non-mystery set aboard a ship, and similarly "Operation Virtual Reality" is simply about a plan that goes awry. A blind woman escapes a murder attempt in "End Matter." This is an entertaining collection but the blurb writers would have you believe that it is a collection of Sloan stories, when he actually only appears in three of the twenty-two.

In some ways Aird writes in the well established tradition of the detective story, although most of the time her novels are more properly considered police procedurals. Her recurring characters do not change in any way over the course of their careers. Sloan is as insecure and deferential as ever in the later books as he was to start with and although he had become a father during the interim, it's little more than an aside and the boy never makes an appearance. Crosby is still a bumbling rookie forty years after his first appearance. Except for one novel and a few short stories, Aird never tried a different protagonist, and even the non-Sloan shorts generally involve minor characters from the main series.

PATRICIA MOYES

Patricia Moyes was the pseudonym used by Patricia Pakenham-Walsh (1923-2000), who worked for Peter Ustinov as his technical assistant for several years before becoming a full time writer. She wrote for both the stage and screen and earned enough to turn to full time writing in 1959. Most of her subsequent books were detective novels, one of which was nominated for the Edgar. She later moved to the Virgin Islands. Most of the best of her work came in the first half of her career. Her detective is Inspector Henry Tibbett, who is sometimes ably assisted by his wife Emmy.

Her first novel was *Dead Men Don't Ski* (1959), which introduced the Tibbetts, whom we meet while they are en route to a skiing vacation in Italy. Among their fellow passengers are Colonel Buckfast and his fussy wife, Jimmy Passendell, a young man who works in finance, and two of the latter's friends who are introduced later. A brief exchange between Henry and Emmy warns the reader that Henry is on assignment despite the trappings of vacation. Interpol believes the hotel to which they are all bound is the center for a smuggling operation, probably drugs, and has asked him to keep his eyes open.

On the cross channel ferry they meet Caro Whittaker and Roger Staines, the young couple traveling together with Passendell. On the final leg of their journey they meet the Baroness von Wurtburg, who unaccountably seems concerned that they are all headed for the same ski resort. It is very clear that the Baroness, who has two young sons, is not happily married. Her husband is not traveling with her and the children are already at the resort. They are accompanied by their governess, Gerda.

The varied party finally reaches the lodge, which is only accessible by chairlift. There Henry makes note of Fritz Hauser, who is clearly not there for the skiing and who meets privately with the resort's proprietor. They also meet Franco, a young Italian who tries to flirt with the baroness. Giulio, the best of the ski instructors, was killed in a skiing accident only a few days before their arrival, which is a shock to those who knew him from previous visits. Also resident are the Knipfers, a man and his wife and their grown daughter who are visiting from Germany.

The first day passes uneventfully except that Staines is seen having tea with Hauser and Whittaker announces that she is in love with their instructor, Pietro. The baroness and Franco seem mildly worried about Hauser for reasons unknown, but their flirtation is now obvious to everyone. Moyes then uses foreshadowing by mentioning that there is an "impending disaster."

Days pass and Hauser announces that he is checking out. But when he arrives at the base of the chairlift he is slumped unnaturally and Henry is there to determine that he is in fact dead of a gunshot wound. Everyone except Henry, Emmy, and Pietro were at the resort, and the chairlift was manned at both ends. The proprietor is also down below, waiting for someone in the local tavern. The baroness' husband shows up at the tavern only minutes after the body is discovered.

Back at the resort, Henry announces Hauser's death and the older Knipfer involuntarily expresses her relief before being hustled away by her husband. Carol Whittaker also fails to conceal her please at the news and refuses to explain. Hauser was apparently shot while descending by someone in one of the ascending cars, which eliminates only the Knipfers. Henry confers with the Italian police and it is clear that he and they both believe Hauser was involved with drugs. He was, as it turns out, a licensed physician who practiced in Italy but who has recently retired.

There are at this point a great many possibilities. Hauser may have been murdered by his confederates for reasons unknown. He may have been blackmailing the Knipfers. He may have reported the baroness and her boyfriend to the domineering husband. He had also aroused the ire of Whittaker for reasons not yet revealed. The police also tell Henry that Hauser was involved in the overdose death of a young Italian actress, which provides yet another motive. Or these could all be red herrings disguising the real reason why he was killed.

The Italian police also mention that Staines' small yacht was apprehended smuggling three years earlier. The crew insisted that Staines had hired them for the job but Staines countered that his boat had been stolen and his story had prevailed. One of the smugglers from that case is a known associate of Hauser, which revelation put the police on the doctor's trail. Certain cash payments into his account suggest blackmail as well. Because the local detective does not speak good English, he asks that Henry attend the interviews, and Emmy ends up being brought as well to take notes in shorthand.

As if we did not already have enough suspects, the proprietor seems to be very uneasy about the payment of Hauser's bill and his business at the resort. During the interviews, Gerda reveals that she held Hauser responsible for the deaths of her parents during the war, providing still another motive, although she denies that she actually killed him or even intended to do so. The Italian police detective – who is not portrayed in particularly favorable terms although he turns up as a friend in one of the later novels – immediately jumps to the conclusion that she is guilty. This, naturally, means she is innocent, and Henry cautions him not to be premature.

Staines reveals that he organized this particular trip with his companions in response to a letter from Hauser suggesting they meet to discuss a business deal. He contends that Hauser then produced a forged note which implicated Staines in a smuggling operation and tried to blackmail him. He produces the letter which he obtained from Hauser. Meanwhile Henry discovers that the Italian detective has been withholding information from him and is not pleased.

Mrs. Buckfast becomes a viable suspect when she confesses that she has been smuggling drugs for Hauser, although she insists she intended to contact the police in England. She was afraid that Hauser was going to eliminate her as unreliable and was therefore quite pleased when he was killed. Although this provides her with an excellent motive, she was not on the chairlift and it does not seem possible that she could have fired the murder weapon. On the other hand, Passendell was the first person to pass Hauser during the ride and Hauser was already slumped over, so he may have been dead already.

Predictably, Hauser was also spying on the baroness and Franco, providing them with a motive. He had documented their affair and given it to the proprietor to hold for the baron when he arrived, but someone – possibly Franco – stole the envelope shortly before Hauser was killed. Henry has a bit of luck at this point. He suspects – as is obvious to the reader – that the proprietor of the hotel knew about Hauser's smuggling operation, even if he disagreed with it. He notices a picture on the man's desk of a young woman and recognizes her as the actress who died of a drug overdose. He confronts the man who admits that she was his daughter and that he was being blackmailed by Hauser who knew that he had sometimes helped her acquire the drugs to which she was addicted. This adds another to the list of suspects and, since he now confesses having voluntarily given Hauser's documents to Franco, it worsens the case against the Italian.

Other potential suspects are Colonel Buckfast, who may have learned about Hauser's suborning of his wife, the Knipfers' daughter, who was supposed to marry Hauser and claims to have welcomed the match, although her demeanor suggests otherwise, and Caro Whittaker, who still hasn't explained why she was so delighted when news of Hauser's murder was announced. It is even possible that Pietro and his father Marco were somehow involved, because Giulio died making a dangerous ski trip across the border into Austria, which might have been at Hauser's urging in order to deliver another shipment of contraband.

Shortly after the half way mark, Henry examines a timetable provided by the Italian police. He then tells Emmy that by looking at the time table, and recalling the remarks made by the various guests, he has figured out the solution. This is the famous challenge to the reader that Ellery Queen employed, though not as bluntly stated. Moyes even tells us that the crucial comment was made by Colonel Buckfast.

At this point Moyes throws in a nice curve ball. The note implicating Staines in the earlier smuggling incident is proven to be a forgery. But the handwriting of the forged note does match someone in the party – Caro Whittaker. And Gerda reports that she saw Staines clandestinely leaving Hauser's room on the day he was murdered. Henry is expecting Mario to come to him as soon as the chairlift closes and provide the final bit of information, but someone murders Mario before he can do so.

The last quarter of the book relies on a standard detective story device. Henry knows who the murderer is – though the reader does not – but he can't reveal the name because he has no evidence, and in the second case he doesn't even know how the murder was done since the time table suggests that no one on the chairlift could have killed Mario while he was descending without being seen. There is a clue to the first murder, however, which readers may have overlooked. Hauser was very familiar with the chairlift and no longer used the safety bar. But when his body was found, the safety bar was in place. This obviously means that he was already dead when he was placed on the lift. The only person who could have done that was Mario, who was stationed at the top. He was convinced that Hauser was responsible for his older son's death – killed making a dangerous smuggling run into Austria. The second murder was therefore obviously the act of someone else, and while the motive is a bit of a stretch, the method is quite nicely worked out.

For a first novel, this was particularly impressive. The fairly large cast of characters are all nicely differentiated and Moyes avoids presenting us with a bewildering list of suspects that are merely interchangeable names. The incremental events leading to the conclusion are logically worked out, Henry solves the case logically. There is some withheld information right at the end, but there is only an exciting ski chase intervening before all is revealed. The active participation of Emmy in the investigation is also an asset and there are at least token attempts to replicate this in the books that followed.

Moyes followed up with *Down Among the Dead Men* (1961, aka *The Sunken Sailor*). Once again the Tibbetts are on vacation, this time boating with their friends, the Bensons, Rosemary and Alastair. To this purpose they travel to Berrybridge Haven, where they are introduced to the harbor master, Herbert Hole and a local boatman named Hamish Rawnsley. Rawnsley has recently come into money following the death of a relative in a boating accident, and Hole is somewhat caustic about it. Hole also makes a vaguely disparaging remark about another local, Sir Simon Trigg-Willoughby. Another local, Bill Hawkes, works maintaining the boats, but Hole considers him incompetent and lazy or both. The Bensons explain that the two men are competitors and that Hawkes actually does good work.

The plan is to sail in company with three other boats, one owned by David Crowther, the fourth by Colin Street and Anne Petrie, who are engaged but not married. The Bensons provide some background information and Henry remembers that Sir Simon's house was burgled by a jewel thief a while back. His sister Priscilla suffers from mild dementia. Neither of them are married.

On their first day of sailing, Alastair tells him the story of Pete Rawnsley's death. Pete was Hamish's uncle and was reputedly the finest sailor in the group. All five boats had been sailing north the previous year when Pete went aground on a sandbar and was forced to wait several hours for the tide to rise. The rest of the party continued northward. A heavy fog moved in, however, and they all lost sight of one another. When it cleared they sailed back and found Pete dead, drowned in a few inches of water, with a bruise on the side of his head and blood on the edge of the boom. The presumption was that he was knocked unconscious when the boom shifted unexpectedly and drowned before regaining consciousness. If this was murder – as the reader will certainly assume – it appears that all of the named characters had the opportunity except possibly Priscilla, who was at home, and Sir Simon, who was out of town.

Henry immediately points out inconsistencies in the story, based largely on the lack of wind and the likelihood that the boom would have been secured. The sandbar was easily accessible by dinghy or motorboat, so even Priscilla must be added to the suspect list since she would have been able to see the sandbar from the house.

Alastair is eager for Henry to investigate but Rosemary is not. He mentions that Pete had been flirting with Anne and that Colin didn't like it. There was a serious argument about it the night before Pete was killed and Anne had been angry enough that she had sailed with David rather than Colin, leaving him alone in his own boat. Anyone could have rowed across from one of the other four boats on the night in question and the fog would have concealed everything. Anne tells Henry that – appearances to the contrary – she and Hamish were probably the only ones who actually liked Pete.

At this point there are several potential motives. Colin was jealous about Anne's affection for Peter. Hamish stood to inherit a considerable amount of money. David mentions something about Pete being disloyal and threatening to expose a slightly illegal but "harmless" business which probably involved himself. Additionally Rosemary is oddly reluctant to talk about the entire affair, Anne suggests that she knows something shady about Herbert Hole, and Hole says the same thing about Sir Simon.

Nothing of consequence occurs for a while, but then the local pub owner, Bob Calloway, returns from a trip and Henry recognizes him as a man once strongly suspected of being a fence for stolen merchandise. Henry also meets George Riddle, who works for Sir

Simon in the house but whose father was an experienced boatman. Sir Simon also mentions that he noticed that Pete Rawnsley had gone aground before he left on his trip, and that he was surprised and even wondered if he had done it deliberately for some arcane reason.

Calloway tells everyone that Henry is a police officer, which causes some changes of attitude. Crowther takes him aside and confides that he and Anne rowed over to the sandbar that day to find Pete, that he heard Pete and Hamish arguing about money and returned without announcing himself. Anne, theoretically, did not hear them at all. Colin indicates that Pete had just rejected Anne and that she had been furious with him, providing her with a motive. He also claims, without being specific, that Pete had threatened to reveal information which would have caused Herbert to lose his position as harbor master. Colin asks if Henry has enough suspects yet. "Not for a really ingenious detective story."

Meanwhile, Rosemary advises Emily that Anne is a vamp and that she's afraid Alastair is falling for him. She also implies that she thinks Anne might have killed Pete for breaking things off with her. This seems to be confirmed when Anne flirts with Henry, but she also tells him a very different story about the trip to the sandbar. She says that David stayed in the dinghy while she went looking for Pete, that she found him, and that he was in a bad moodn because he had just had an accident and hit himself in the head with the boom.

Moyes ratchets up the tension at this point. Herbert Hole appears to have been elected as the new mayor, and his acceptance speech includes caustic remarks about Pete Rawnsley, Bill Hawkes, and others. Colin and Hamish decide to embarrass the harbor master and point out that something was wrong with the vote count since the total exceeds the number of voters. A recount proves that Hawkes was actually elected, and Hole vows to get even with the two "troublemakers." A short time later Colin publicly announces that he knows Pete was murdered and intends to prove it.

Since Colin is practically begging to be murdered, it is no surprise that his body is discovered floating nearby on the following morning. He has drowned and his dinghy is found floating capsized a short distance away. The postmortem indicates that he was rendered unconscious by a blow to the head prior to drowning. Based on an account in a book which Colin had mentioned, Henry concludes that the missing jewels were buried on the sandbar.

Emmy meanwhile has been talking to Priscilla alone at her home when someone overhears them. The car which was meant to take her back is sent away because the drive is told that she had already gone. Henry immediately realizes that she is in danger. For a while we are meant to believe that Sir Simon abducted Emmy, and for a briefer period it appears to have been Crowther. Priscilla is found unconscious, having taken or been given an overdose of sleeping pills and soon dies. Crowther finds the missing jewels buried on the sandbar and Henry lays a trap that eventually leads to the arrest of Sir Simon.

There are a great many parallels between the two novels, in addition to both taking place during vacation trips. In both cases, a presumed accident attracts Henry's attention as a possible murder in disguise. These murders have taken place long before the actual story begins. In both cases the local police are unimaginative. Marital infidelity is a common element as is the insular setting with its distrust of outsiders. A book proves to be a crucial piece of evidence introduced toward the end in each of them. The second murder is necessary because someone threatens to reveal the person responsible for the first.

The identity of the killer is mildly telegraphed in this one. The scene in which we are supposed to accept that Sir Simon was working for an extended period of time not far from where Emmy was lying tied and gagged is just not convincing. The summing up is complete and well arranged. This was marginally better than her first novel.

The Tibbetts returned in *Death on the Agenda* (1962). Henry is in Geneva attending a conference dealing with international drug smuggling. He is part of a subcommittee with includes Jacques Lenoir from France, Alfred Spezzi – the Italian police officer whom Henry met in *Dead Men Don't Ski*, Bill Parkington from the US, Juan Moranta from Spain, and Konrad Zwemmer of West Germany. We are also introduced to two translators, John Trapp and Helene Brochet. Emmy meanwhile is being entertained by an old friend, Annette Delacroix. She is also working for the conference and is romantically involved with John Trapp.

The subcommittee members are all invited to a party at the home of expatriate Americans Paul and Natasha Hampton. Parkington takes Henry aside and tells him that someone is leaking confidential information from the conference and the subcommittee, including the agenda which was known only to the six members, two translators, a secretary, and a recording clerk, Mary Benson. During the course of the party, Henry is inadvertently present when Paul Hampton observes Trapp emerging from his wife's bedroom. Parkington suspects that Trapp is the leak because of his onetime membership in the Communist Party.

The subcommittee is set to meet in a suite or secured rooms the following morning. Trapp arrives early, chases everyone out of the small office, and begins to type, announcing that he needs to talk to Henry as soon as he arrives. Henry hears the typing but deals with some other brief issues before entering the office. There he finds Trapp dead, stabbed to death with an ornamental knife that they had all seen at the Hampton estate. The document he had been typing refers to Henry as having missed an appointment with Trapp – none had been made – and begins to express what appears to be a response to Parkington's implications. Much to Henry's annoyance, the others all suspect him since he was the one who found the body.

Emmy meanwhile has discovered that Natasha and John were occasionally seen together in public, and that she had introduced him as her husband. The police find a note from Trapp in the pocket of Henry's overcoat acknowledging that they had a meeting, which was obviously planted. Convinced that he must prove his own innocence rather than rely on the Swiss police, Henry goes to Trapp's apartment where he learns that the dead man received the note about the meeting at seven that morning, that a written acknowledgment was requested, and that it had been delivered by a woman who spoke French.

Moyes, through Henry, warns us that there are two people involved, one man and one woman. None of the women could have put the note in Henry's pocket and the men could not have delivered the message. This complicates rather than simplifies the issue. He also eliminates Annette from consideration because of her evident grief, and because she was not working with them when the initial leak was made. They also turn up a connection between Zwemmer and Benson, but it seems too early in the book for this to be a significant discovery.

Armed with photographs of the women, Henry tries to get Trapp's landlady to identify which one delivered the message, but she has suddenly moved away because of an "accident" in the family. Natasha confesses that her marriage to Paul is a sham and that he knows and even approves of her affairs, so long as she is discreet.

A small but interesting point emerges during this conversation. Since Paul was in Paris, Natasha spent the night in John's apartment. She was present when he responded to the message, but insisted that she didn't know what it was about. That suggests that the note found in the typewriter at the murder scene might not have been written by the victim, might have been planted as part of the effort to frame Henry. He also learns that Parkington is not good about keeping a secret and that the other members of the group may all have known about the leak – and the fact that it had been discovered - prior to the murder. It also appears from the guard's testimony that Moranta could not have killed Trapp because he arrived just in time to find Henry with the body, although he may have been the male half of the duo.

Henry, who is flirting with Mary, constructs a strong case against Annette and an unnamed male, but admits that he doubts if it is true. Brochet implies that she is more than she seems to be and shortly after Henry mentions that the landlady might be able to identify the messenger, the landlady and her entire family are killed in what is obviously a staged accident.

There is another exciting ending as Emmy is held captive and forced to lure Henry into a trap. There are lots of red herrings and one surprise - there actually was only one traitor inside the group. The fact that the typed note was much too short to have taken more than half an hour to type is not necessarily obvious, particularly to non-typists, and might be dismissed as author error, although it is not. There is also a rather subtle instance of the killer revealing knowledge that she should not have learned. Hampton's involvement is obvious but the nature of that involvement is not. All of the clues this time are right out in the open, but it is quite a job to assemble them all and come up with a solution.

Murder a la Mode (1963) opens in the offices of a fashion magazine managed by Margery French. Her immediate staff includes Patrick Walsh, Teresa Manners, Donald MacKay, Olwen Piper, Helen Pankhurst, photographer Michael Healey, and the secretary Rachel Field. Godfrey Goring is the chief shareholder in the magazine; he is married to former actress Lorna Vincent. The staff is under pressure because the semi-annual Paris fashion show issue is always a last minute project because of the timing of the Parisians.

Margery's health is failing and she is trying decide who should be her successor. Manners has a better sense of fashion but Pankhurst is much more suited to be an administrator. The board of trustees favors Pankhurst but Margery knows that Manners would leave the magazine rather than work for her, and her flair for fashion is indispensible.

The late session ends and everyone except Pankhurst leaves, most of them invited out for a drink by Goring. Healy, Field, and Manners had just returned from Paris and their suitcases have been left in the offices. Pankhurst discovers that one of them is unlocked and opens it, searching for some object whose nature is concealed from the reader. She finds it and removes it. The following morning, the messenger service arrives to pick up the finished copy, but no one answers the bell and when the doorman finally arrives, he finds Pankhurst dead.

Henry Tibbett is called to the scene, and there is a slight personal connection because his niece is a model who was doing some work for the magazine. Pankhurst was poisoned, presumably by something placed in her tea. Margery French is the first to be interviewed and she reveals that Pankhurst had been having an unhappy love affair with Healy, and that Healy is married to Manners. Piper, who roomed with Pankhurst, tells Henry that she was pregnant.

The next few revelations are fascinating. Manners insists that her husband's relationship with Pankhurst was completely platonic outside of some mild flirting and that it didn't bother her at all. Healy initially denies it, but when Henry mentions that the dead woman was pregnant, he confesses to the affair. But then the medical examiner tells Henry that not only was Pankhurst not pregnant, she was still a virgin. Nicholas Knight, a designer who was with Goring on the night of the murder, is oddly upset when asked if he attended the shows in Paris, but won't explain.

Predictably, the niece decides to investigate on her own. She discovers and tells Henry that one of the office keys has gone missing. He runs into a dead end trying to trace Pankhurst's visits to a "doctor" mentioned in her diary, so the trips to the country must have been for a different reason. Walsh provides the explanation. Pankhurst was in love with a married man.. She had taken him to a doctor and convinced the doctor to tell her the results by posing as the man's wife. The man has incurable cancer and less than a year to live. Although rumor would have it that the man was Healy, it seems much more likely that it was Goring. Walsh also reveals that he is secretly married to French, although they have been separated for decades.

Henry is close to a crucial clue. He believes that someone stole the key to the office so that they could return after Pankhurst was dead and steal something from one of the suitcases. Unfortunately, Pankhurst accidentally opened Field's suitcase so he assumes that was where the mysterious item was hidden, and the only person who could have had access to that was his niece. The reader knows that it was actually in one of the other two cases, but had been removed by Pankhurst. Its present whereabouts are unknown.

Once again predictably, the niece disappears, lured away by a faked telegram, and no one knows where to find her. She turns up, surprisingly, at a fashion show, having been located off stage by Henry and enlisted in a plan to expose the killers - Field and Knight - who are actually brother and sister. Goring was indeed Pankhurst's lover, but Healy was pretending to fill that role in order to conceal the relationship from Goring's wife. The murderous couple was actually stealing exclusive designs from Paris and Pankhurst had inadvertently stumbled onto the method and evidence of what was going on.

Moyes obviously veered away from her pattern this time. The Tibbetts are not traveling and they don't appear at all in the opening chapter. Henry's refusal to listen to his niece when she tells him she has important information is startlingly out of character, a device designed to fuel that subplot but inconsistent with what we know about his methods. The resolution includes a small piece of withheld information – the stolen key was so large that it must certainly have been missed earlier than when it was reported – but otherwise builds its case incrementally and logically from a fairly large number of clues presented within the story.

Falling Star (1964) is a further departure from the pattern of the earlier novels. It is narrated in first person by Anthony Croombe-Peters, better known as Pudge, the man in charge of finances for a movie production company working on its first project. Keith Pardoe is the set designer and Bridget Brennan, his wife, wrote the screenplay. The director is Sam Potman, assisted rather ineptly by Gervase Mountjoy, and the lead actors are Bob Meakin and Fiametta Fettini. The latter's husband is Giulio Pallado. Louise Cohen is the production manager and Margery Phipps is responsible for continuity.

Fettini becomes infatuated with Meakin and eventually there is a major fight on set in the subway. One scene has to be redone unexpectedly because the previous film was spoiled, and in the process Meakin falls in front of the train and is killed, apparently the result of an accident as he stumbled just as he reached the platform. The film company was insured for such a contingency and in fact came out ahead of the game and able to reshoot the movie with a different lead. It turns out that Meakin secretly had a wife named Sonia, whose existence was suppressed because he was a more appealing figure as a bachelor.

There are a couple of minor puzzles already. Potman disappears for the afternoon following the accident and never explains where he was. His personality is alternately abrasive and ingratiating and it is impossible to determine which facet is genuine. Pardoe impersonates Pudge and announces that Fettini will give an interview, which Pudge opposes vehemently because of her irresponsibility. Various other problems hold up shooting for over a month, during which – through a fairly logical sequence of events – Pardoe is chosen to replace Meakin even though he has had no previous experience as an actor.

After Fettini unfairly accuses her of theft, Phipps resigns without notice. A few days later she falls to her death from her apartment balcony, apparently a suicide. There is a not very specific suicide note. Pudge, who knows Henry Tibbett socially, tries to enlist his aid in suppressing any possible bad publicity, but Henry is not in a position to help. Until almost the halfway point in the novel, he has still not made an actual appearance.

Tibbett has been made aware of some inconsistencies in Phipps' background and that her father was an occasional blackmailer. She also sent a note to her birth mother, as opposed to her foster mother, on the day of her death suggesting that she was on the verge of some big deal. Henry suspects that she was blackmailing someone involved with the film and may have been murdered and tries, unsuccessfully, to enlist Pudge's help.

There are clear tensions among the main characters. Pardoe has become insufferable since becoming an actor and his wife, Brennan, is an emotional wreck. Potman continues to be insincerely friendly alternating with spells of rudeness and inconsistency. This begins to come to a boil when Henry announces that Phipps' suicide note was a forgery and that she had been murdered, pushed through the kitchen window rather than falling from the balcony as was previously assumed.

Henry points out that Sonia Meakin mentioned Phipps' connection with the movie even though there was no apparent way that she could have known. Sonia contacts Pudge, admits that she knew Phipps well enough to have visited her, and suggests there was something strange about her husband's "accident." She also asserts that since Meakin had intended to break his contract, he was no longer an employee and the insurance should not have been paid. That's a very dubious contention because intent is not assertion and in any case he would still technically have been an employee until the lawsuit was settled.

Pudge is led to believe that there is further evidence of Meakin having quit concealed somewhere in Phipps' apartment, so he convinces the landlord to let him in, but before he can find the documents, Phipps' birth mother – Mrs. Arbuthnot – shows up and demands to know why he is there. He also has guessed that Phipps was blackmailing Sonia Meakin, who similarly wants access to the apartment. This seems to eliminate her as the murderer since she could have taken whatever she was looking for on the day that Phipps died.

The plot thickens when Potman comes to Pudge and tells him that Murray, the man who used to dress Meakin, has turned up dead on his doorstep, his head bashed in. Potman concealed the body and wants Pudge to help him to relocate it. The decision by both men to do so is decidedly implausible. Fortunately someone else discovers the body before they can do so, which only makes them look even more guilty. Potman claims to have been out and Henry appears to accept his version of events. Then Potman mentions a black box and a pair of spectacles to Pudge, without explaining the significance of either.

Sonia contends that someone substituted clear glasses for the prescription ones her husband wore and that this was why he stumbled and fell in front of the train. This is rather a stretch as a method of murdering someone, particularly since they hadn't even known that they would need to reshoot that particular scene, a point which Henry makes later on. Sonia claims that Murray realized this and was blackmailing her – which doesn't make sense because it would have had no effect on her insurance settlement – and that he was probably also blackmailing Potman, which also doesn't make sense since Murray knew that Potman had no money. Sonia Meakin claims to have gone to see Potman, noticed the slumped body through the door, and anonymously called the police, which also seems implausible. It is also inconceivable that the insurance company would not have wanted to view the film showing the accident, and that no one else would even have looked at it.

The use of a first person narrator allows us to see Henry through another, and rather egocentric, point of view, but it requires that excuses be found for him to be present during key conversations with the other characters, which is not always convincingly done. Additionally there are severe problems with inconsistent characterization, plausible situations, and a legal plot element that Moyes appears to have misconstrued or misunderstood. There is also a great deal of withheld information; Henry was actually the instigator of several acts by other people and was privy to a great deal of information that was not available to the reader. It was the first of her novels to be disappointing, but unfortunately it would not be the last.

Johnny Under Ground (1965) opens with Emmy Tibbett deciding to attend a reunion of people like her who served at a military station in Dymfield during World War II. The reunion has been arranged by Arthur Price, the former equipment officer. Emmy was at the time romantically involved with "Beau" Guest, a married man, and close friends with Annie Day and Lofty Parker. Also attending are Jimmy Baggott and Vere Prendergast, the latter of whom married Beau's widow, Barbara. There are some hard feelings between Baggott, who became very successful, and Parker, whose fortunes have not been as lofty as his name.

During the course of the reunion, Moyes reveals that Beau is believed to have committed suicide after his face was badly scarred in an air crash. On the day of his death, Beau planned to secretly replace Vere as pilot of a new aircraft as part of a bet. The pilot on that flight cut off all contact and flew directly out to sea, never to be seen or heard from again. Although officially an accident, the group personally believed that he had committed suicide either because of Barbara's affairs with other men or because of his disfigurement, but Emmy feels that he believed himself to be a failure and just didn't want to live any longer.

Barbara suggests that Baggott write a history of their unit and he agrees, but only if Emmy is willing to do the necessary research. The book evolves into a biography of Beau and there is an interesting series of scenes alternating between flashbacks and Barbara's reconstruction of events to make herself look better. Emmy senses that there is something going on that is hidden from her and Henry attempts to get her to withdraw from the project until Vere presses him to do so. That makes him suspicious that there is in fact something which needs to be unearthed.

Tension grows when Lofty speculates about the reasons for Beau's suicide, if it was suicide. Even Henry is beginning to have suspicions. Vere is disproportionately upset by the discussion and threatens to withhold the financing his wife offered, but Baggott is now interested enough to carry on anyway.

Emmy goes to see Sammy Smith, another member of the group, who didn't attend the reunion. Smith admits quite frankly that he thought Beau was arrogant before his accident and unbalanced afterward. Annie Day is defensive and even hostile to the whole idea, and she suggests that there is a possibility that Beau is still alive. Baggott also admits disliking Beau, but insists that he respected him as well. Next is Beau's father, a retired minister, who turns out to be a self obsessed snob who never had an emotional connection with his son.

Vere offers to pay to have a lawyer vet the manuscript and Baggott, who works in television, hints about buying the rights in advance of publication, which Parker suspects might be in order to suppress rather than publicize the book. Parker is then killed, found dead in a sealed room with the gas on, but Emmy convinces Henry to take a closer look and they determine that he was murdered and his notebooks removed from the house.

Henry launches a secretive investigation after allowing the press to believe that it was indeed a suicide. Since he believes that Emmy is another potential victim, he insists that she accompany him, which provides a neatly plausible way to include her in the main action that follows. The illusion of suicide seems unnecessary since Henry's subsequent questioning of all the parties would certainly tell them that the police suspected foul play.

His first interview is with Arthur Price, who has a lengthy but unconfirmable alibi. Henry suspects the man is lying and proves it when a critical part of the story is found to be untrue. Annie Day is completely uncooperative and Baggott appears determined to pursue the story on his own as a possible property for a television production. Barbara wants the project to move forward and claims that Vere supports her, although this would contradict his previously expressed opinion.

Henry visits the old airfield and finds Beau's skeleton in one of the air raid bunkers, with a revolver in one hand. It appears that his father knew that he was there. Vere goes off with Emmy and then comes to see Henry alone, vaguely asserting that Emmy is with Barbara. Later he says that Emmy has gone off with another man, identity unknown. This is all designed to suggest that Emmy is in peril, but it's all a red herring. The coroner reports that Beau's head wound was not self inflicted; he was probably murdered. An unknown woman has called and stirred up the father, an anonymous letter has been sent to Smith, and Henry can't locate any of them when he tries to find his wife.

Vere takes advantage of the confused situation to go see Henry, at which point he claims that he actually piloted the lost plane but bailed out and walked back, primarily to protect Beau's reputation with Barbara, whom he also loved. Price showed up and offered to take Emmy home but instead has taken her to a party at Baggott's house. Annie Day and Sammy Smith are there as well. They collectively suggest that they think Emmy murdered Beau. There is a slight clue to the truth here as everyone received blackmail letters which they concealed from the police, except Smith who turns his over to Henry. This suggests correctly that he was the blackmailer and included himself to throw the police off the scent.

Another element of the story has to this point been limited to hints. Beau's mother ran off with another man but became an alcoholic and has been institutionalized for years. She had a son – name unknown – by her lover, who left her shortly after the boy was born. That son, Beau's half-brother, was Lofty Parker. Barbara, meanwhile, admits that she has been receiving letters supposedly from Beau, which would invalidate her marriage to Vere and her access to his considerable wealth, since Beau was never officially declared dead. These developments explain all of the falsehoods and withheld testimony.

    This was a decided improvement from the previous book and is an excellent example of the cold case mystery, one in which an old death is proved to be murder and solved years after the fact. It is well constructed, complex, and devious. It does seem a bit of a stretch that the body could have remained undiscovered in an air raid bunker from 1943 to the present, but it is not a major plot point.

    Murder Fantastical (1967) opens with a rather odd call from George Manciple to his neighbor, the Chief Constable, to tell him that another neighbor – Raymond Mason - with whom he has been feuding has been found shot to death in his driveway. Mason had been harassing George and Violet Manciple for some time, for reasons unknown, but had made a friendly visit that day. Upon leaving, his car had unaccountably stopped partway down the driveway. Mason got out, cried out in apparent terror, and was shot dead. The only witness was Dora Manciple, George's elderly aunt. The murder weapon, a pistol, was found in the nearby shrubbery wiped clean of fingerprints. The car stopped because of an anti-theft device, which had presumably been activated by the killer.

    The Manciples are having a family get together. Included are Edwin Manciple, a retired bishop, and their own daughter Maud, who is accompanied by Julian Manning-Richards, her boyfriend. There is also Sir Claud and Lady Romana Manciple. All of the Manciples are larger than life characters verging on caricatures, but by intent. It appears that Mason was trying to woo Maud despite the large difference in their ages and the presence of her boyfriend. He also has an adult son, Frank, whom none of the other characters have ever met.

    Mason was determined to buy the Manciple house, apparently because he was insulted by the local people refusing to accept him as a landed gentleman. George Manciple can barely make ends meet because his father invested his money poorly and because the family jewels were apparently replaced by glass imitations and sold. Mason's latest tactic had been to pursue Maud, and he had had a violent argument with Julian.

Frank Mason turns up within hours of his father's death, which is suspicious in itself. He insists that Julian killed him but Julian reveals that Frank – whom he knows from their university days together – had once claimed that he would cheerfully kill his own father if he thought he could get away with it. Mason Senior was threatening to claim nepotism since Julian was in the running for a job as secretary to one of the Manciple brothers, and Julian himself disappears for several hours without explanation, and later claims he made an urgent trip to London and back, but won't explain why, although there is evidence later suggesting that it was unrelated. This turns out to be a double red herring.

Mason ran a legal bookmaking company, which Henry visits. There he learns that Mason had a number of private clients, off the company records, one of whom is Sir John Adamson, another neighbor, who was presently heavily in debt to Mason, at least according to a secret account book. Sir John, however, insists that he owes no money and that the accounts were faked as a potential weapon against him. Henry has by this point indicated that he does not expect to make an arrest in the case, but he won't explain why.

Henry finds one of Manciple's handguns, which he had recently reported missing, hidden in the attic of Mason's cottage. When Dora Manciple dies, everyone assumes it was because of her advanced age, but Henry suspects that she was helped along. He confronts Frank Mason about the gun, which Mason admits finding but says is now missing. It is obvious that he has been searching the cottage for something, but Henry has anticipated him and points out that a specific book is missing without revealing how he knew that it would be that particular volume. Frank, it appears, has also fallen for Maud.

Henry explains that Mason's death was an accident, that he had rigged what was supposed to be a near miss, but broke cover when Dora came outside to warn her off, accidentally placing himself in line for the fatal shot. This was to be part of his plan to drive the Manciples out of their house. Henry posits two questions. Why was Mason so determined to own the property? Who killed

Dora Manciple and why? The first is pretty clearly connected to the missing family jewels – presumed sold – because Moyes would not have spent so much time telling us about them if they were not to become significant later on. They were undoubtedly concealed someplace in the house, although no one knows where. There are also the subsidiary questions of the whereabouts of the gun and the missing book.

The Manciples are sponsoring a party open to the public and during the confusion, someone returns the missing firearm to where it belongs. Henry is called away by Mason's business manager, who says the private files have been stolen – and that he believes Frank Mason was the thief. This turns out to be true, but to his credit Frank is destroying the incriminating files.

There have been hints all along that Julian was not the person he claimed to be, an orphan of British residents in a newly independent African nation. Henry is able to figure out the subterfuge by having the police review certain newspapers published at critical periods. There is a rather frenetic ending – Julian is unmasked as a spy and the family jewels are recovered. Moyes would later use the false identity device to much better effect in *Who Is Simon Warwick?*

This was Moyes' first attempt at broad humor. The Manciple family consists of highly eccentric people and the dialogue is frequently quite funny. Although Emmy accompanies Henry during this particular investigation, she is almost entirely off stage and incidental to the plot. The novel is much more successful as a comic novel than as a mystery, chiefly because the Manciples are such an interesting and unconventional family. Moyes included cameo appearances of some family members occasionally in later books.

Death and the Dutch Uncle (1968) opens with the death of a small time crook and gambler named Byers, shot and left for dead in the bathroom of a seedy bar called the Pink Parrot which is patronized by other criminals and which is run by Major Weatherby, who found the body. Henry has recently been promoted to Superintendent and is assigned the case. Byers died muttering "145" and the name Madeleine, his current girlfriend. He also mentions a horse named "Phil" or something similar, as he had become delirious and hard to understand by that point. Madeleine is introduced as Weatherby's niece, but Henry doubts that is true.

Both Weatherby and Madeleine stick to their story that a man in obvious disguise and with a fake foreign accent came into the bar, followed Byers into the restroom, and shot him, although no one heard any shots. The bar just happened to empty out of other customers about that time and naturally Weatherby doesn't know any of them by name. To Henry's surprise, another witness turns up – apparently truthful – and confirms their story.

Emmy meanwhile has had a call from Gordon Trapp, brother of the victim in *Death on the Agenda*. Trapp is an interpreter working for an international commission attempting to settle a border dispute between two new African nations. He is troubled by the recent deaths of two commission members, both of whom were clearly leaning in one direction, and says that he suspects another will die soon. The two deceased were both elderly and seem to have died of natural causes but despite his protestation that he sees nothing suspicious in the case, Henry cannot completely discount Trapp's story.

An examination of Byers' bank account reveals that he had deposited a substantial amount of cash shortly before his death. Byers worked odd jobs in hotel kitchens and Henry is inquiring at one when he happens to overhear that one of the two elderly diplomats died in that same hotel, and that his room number was 145. Byers had just recently started work there and his job was to facilitate delivery of trays ordered through room service, and the obvious supposition is that he put poison in the meal delivered to that room.

Henry has Trapp point out to him the key members of the commission who might be targets for assassination. The most likely seems to be Koetsveen, a Dutch national. Trapp also points out the other interpreter, Pierre Malvaux, and the secretary, Yvonne. Henry then finds another connection between the two cases. One of the earlier deaths occurred when an elderly diplomat slipped and fell in front of a bus. The chief witness to the event turns out to be Major Weatherby.

Trapp has a visit from someone from the disputed area in Africa, Honeyman, who saw a small mining operation going on and whose private plane was shot at by the miners. Honeyman disappears under mysterious circumstances before Henry can talk to him and he puts Trapp into protective custody. Honeyman's knapsack turns up empty in a cab, after which Henry discovers that the secretary, Yvonne, has the same last name as Madeleine from the bar. They are sisters and they both have the same story of innocence which Henry cannot pierce. Madeleine then leaves England and goes to Amsterdam while a private plane is stolen to give the appearance that Honeyman voluntarily disappeared. This is all a somewhat clumsy red herring since Honeyman did go into hiding voluntarily, and stole the plane despite the reasoned arguments why it would have made no sense for him to have done that.

Trapp is sent to Holland secretly – although the villains follow him – where he meets with the Tibbetts, who are supposedly on vacation. Unfortunately his habit of ignoring instructions and letting the opposition know where he is makes Trapp useless to Henry's attempt to thwart a plot against Koetsveen, who has returned for a vacation while the committee is in recess. Trapp spots Madeleine and follows her clandestinely, much to Henry's dismay, but he and Emmy arrange for their own temporary disappearance soon afterward.

The Tibbetts approach Koetsveen – the Dutch uncle of the title – who is appropriately rude and uncooperative. Henry subsequently confronts two armed thugs alone and is nearly overwhelmed before Honeyman resurfaces, accompanied by Trapp, in time to save the day – and Koetsveen. There is a very dramatic and action filled ending, with Emmy taken prisoner, Henry getting shot, and various criminals being brought to justice. It was all designed, of course, to alter the outcome of the border commission.

This was Moyes' first effort at real international intrigue and she brings it off quite well, a success she would unfortunately not repeat in later attempts. The plot is just vague enough to be intriguing without being so vague that it's incomprehensible. There is also a kind of cameo appearance by Inspector Van Der Valk, who featured in a series of mystery novels by Nicolas Freeling. There is, in fact, a minor problem with the plot. Since Van Der Valk would necessarily know that a Dutch national was in danger of being assassinated, he would hardly be content to leave the man's protection to a visiting English policeman and his wife. It is also more of an adventure story than a mystery, since we know pretty much who is responsible for the murders and why very early in the story.

Many Deadly Returns (1970) has also been published as *Who Saw Her Die?* and is a variation of the country house murder format. Dr. Edouard Duval and his wife Primrose reluctantly go to England to visit Primrose's mother on her birthday. Also scheduled to attend are her sister Violet and her husband, Piet van der Hoven, and the third sister, Daffodil Swasheimer, and her American husband Charles. Daffodil, who married for money, is having an affair with her husband's son by a previous marriage.

Their mother is Lady Balaclava, a widow who lives with just a companion, Dorothy Underwood-Threep. Lady Balaclava is convinced that an attempt will be made on her life and Henry's superior at Scotland Yard "requests" that he and Emmy accept an invitation to attend her birthday gathering. Lady Balaclava believes that someone is going to try to kill her over the course of the weekend, but the only explanation she offers is that the Ouija board told her so. Shortly after arriving, Henry meets Dr. Griffiths, who is not staying, and learns that Edouard will not be visiting after all. There is a minor mystery because Dorothy, known as Dolly, will not work the Ouija board and Lady Balaclava, who is actually called Crystal, will not admit who has helped her with it in the past.

Henry finds a can of the poisonous spray used in the greenhouse hidden in the back of the cupboard where the birthday presents are stored in preparation for the party. The party begins and even though Henry takes a bit of the cake, sips from Crystal's glass, and even sniffs the flowers before she does, when Crystal does the same she promptly drops dead. Dr. Griffiths has been called away so Dr. Massingham comes in his stead.

The early assumption is that poison from the greenhouse was used to commit the crime, but the autopsy reveals no sign of any poison and the medical opinion is natural causes, a conclusion which Henry immediately rejects. Everyone believes the estate is to be divided equally among the three daughters, with Dolly receiving only a pittance, which would seem to remove her from suspicion, except that Henry hints that this was not a crime committed for financial gain. Only Violet appears to be genuinely grieving. When the will is actually read, the three daughters do receive the proceeds of their father's trust – which constitutes the bulk of the estate – but Crystal had accumulated a smaller fortune of her own, which is bequeathed to Dolly, who faints upon hearing the news.

With no official reason to question a verdict of natural death, Henry is frustrated and vows to resign if he can't solve the case. Dr. Massingham is similarly convinced that it was murder. This seems to be borne out when Dolly falls into a coma and the diagnosis is slow poisoning, possibly by an insecticide. Piet had brought a sample of a new one for Dolly and the package is found opened, although only Dolly and Emmy are believed to have had access to it.

Eventually Henry is led to investigate rumors that Crystal was seriously ill around the time of the war. He discovers that she had tuberculosis and was cured, but the cure may have left her with a violent allergy to streptomycin. Inconsistencies in the stories of Edouard and Primrose crop up, and as a doctor Edouard could have acquired streptomycin, but analysis suggests instead that there may be marital problems behind the conflicting stories rather than a murder plot. There is a nice false solution toward the end, but too much information necessary to solving the mystery is withheld until the climax.

Outwardly this is a fairly traditional mystery and the puzzle is certainly an interesting one. Somehow, despite that, the novel does not really come together. The sisters are almost indistinguishable from one another and a long time passes without any progress at all. When we do receive clues, they are mostly accidental or are provided by outside agencies rather than through Henry's deductive powers. The reversals in the closing chapters are startling but they seem to come out of nowhere and are not dramatically satisfying.

Season of Snows and Sins (1971) repeats the use of a ski resort as its setting, but the story itself is very different. The first few pages are very confusing, bad tactics for a suspense novel. Two different Swiss weddings are talked about simultaneously and it is very hard to keep clear which events are connected to which wedding since the characters are at this point just names rather than people. Giselle Arnay, an actress, is marrying Michel Veron while Robert Drivaz is doing the same with Anne-Marie Durey. Jane Weston, the narrator of the story, is the only foreigner at the latter wedding. Anne-Marie, an orphan employed at the local inn, becomes a model for Weston, who is a sculptor.

At the same time, Bienne – the local real estate agent – is trying to sell an apartment to the Claudets. Pierre Claudet is a minor official in the French government. Anne-Marie and Robert seem doomed to remain apart because his wealthy mother refuses to allow him to marry a penniless orphan and her employer refuses to keep her if she marries. So Weston manages to get them a job as joint concierge of the new apartment building.

Weston invites the Tibbetts to visit her for a skiing vacation, and when they discover that she herself does not ski, they talk her into enrolling in a beginners' ski class. The other member is Sylvie Claudet. The apartment is not ready for occupancy yet so she is staying with Giselle Arnay while her husband attends a conference in Brussels. Weston becomes good friends with the Claudets and their goddaughter, Chantal, but she also becomes aware of the fact that Arnay and Drivaz are being seen together and that they are obviously having some sort of affair. She is also rather puzzled by the status of Mario, who is somewhere between being a servant and a friend in the Arnay-Veron household.

The affair becomes torrid before Drivaz is dumped, after which he becomes abusive and drinks heavily. Then he is stabbed to death in his home and Anne-Marie insists that she was called away and returned to find him dead. But the call, if real, was obviously faked and she is arrested for murder. A fresh snowfall eliminates the possibility of a third party having come and gone, so she is convicted. In view of the circumstances, she is sent to a convent rather than prison, and when she gives birth, the baby is to be adopted by Drivaz's mother.

The Tibbetts return for another visit and Henry inadvertently observes Arnay, Veron, Chantal, and a local ski instructor smoking pot and having group sex. Arnay asks Weston to do a model of her head and Weston is excited about the project. Emmy takes over as the narrator at that point, providing a somewhat different perspective, and a good deal of time is spent repeating the story from her point of view.

Henry becomes convinced that Anne-Marie is innocent. He reads the newspaper accounts of the trial and decides that the defense attorney did not do a proper job. His fees were paid by Sylviea Claudet, anonymously, and it is the testimony of Sylvie – who insists that she did not call from Paris to ask Anne-Marie to clean her apartment – that invalidates the first part of Anne-Marie's alibi, and Weston's insistence that she saw Anne-Marie return to her cottage at five o'clock rather than thirty minutes later that demolishes it. Henry also believes that the trial was flawed because Veron, Arnay, and Chantal were not even questioned – even though Veron was not even in the country at the time. Although this proves to be relevant later, Henry's announcement of it in advance does not seem to follow logically.

Sylvie seems oddly nervous when Henry begins to ask questions about what happened on the day of the murder. She was in Paris, at a conference, and her maid had the day off. Chantal had borrowed the car and obviously could have returned to their apartment and made the phone call or might even have driven to the scene of the crime and back.

Darnay contradicts Sylvie's story that Drival saw her in Paris, and in fact implies that he saw Sylvie instead, and that she is lying because she fears a scandal would affect her husband's career. She is otherwise very uncooperative other than to insist that there was nothing between her and Drival, which is clearly a lie. Henry also talks to Weston and points out that her account of what happened has to be wrong because she insisted that it was raining, which wasn't true. She only thought it was because the figure she saw was huddled under an umbrella, which also means that she could not have positively identified Anne-Marie. This seems quite rudimentary and should have come out in the trial. Moyes appears to have made the defense lawyer unrealistically incompetent simply to allow Henry to take the case apart.

At this point Sylvie becomes the narrator. Sylvie believes that Chantal is a drug addict and worries that she may indeed have lied about where she was on the day of the murder. It is suggested that Arnay was not the killer but that she suspects that one of her acquaintances did it and framed Anne-Marie. Chantal is also clearly hiding something. The role of Mario in these events grows more mysterious and it is suggested that Veron sent him to kill Drival. Other theories offered are that Weston was the killer, or that Sylvie dispatched Chantal to do it.

Emmy returns as narrator. The Tibbetts go to Paris where they discover that Sylvie once worked at a hat shop that was a front for a brothel. Henry discovers that the former owner of the brothel has been blackmailing his old clients and then points out that Sylvie could have flown to Switzerland and back in time to have committed the murders herself. Upon checking further, however, Henry discovers that it was Chantal flew to Switzerland and rented a car, not Sylvie.

The truth slowly emerges. Chantal and Mario were both child prostitutes and knew one another. Mario hated Sylvie because she was instrumental in getting the business closed down. In fact, her husband was the owner and she convinced him that he would be exposed if he didn't anonymously arrange for it to be put out of business. She killed Drivaz because he had learned the truth and was threatening to black mail her.

The solution is generally unsatisfactory. There is withheld information as well as elaborate and unbelievable red herrings. There is no explanation why Veron would have considered murdering Henry, and later tried to bribe him, since he and Arnay are not remotely connected to the crime. Henry says that he was telling the truth about a blackmailer accosting former clients – but that's not true. He attempted to bribe the Claudets, neither of whom was a client. We aren't told that Chantal's passport was missing until the solution is revealed and there is never any explanation of how Sylvie managed to return from the murder scene without leaving tracks in the snow.

Once again the focus is shifted from detection to a more active narrative. Although Moyes did this reasonably well, she was not a strong enough writer to produce a novel of this variety consistently. There are serious problems of pacing – a page and a half are dedicated to explaining how a particular Swiss meal is prepared – and none of the characters except the narrator acquire any real depth. The interesting mystery involving what appears to be an impossible crime is ignored until so late in the story that it seems almost an afterthought, and then it is not explained. The use of multiple narrators to provide different views of the same situation is frequently very entertaining but Moyes repeats too much of the same material.

The Tibbetts are off on vacation again in *The Curious Affair of the Third Dog* (1973). Emmy leaves first to visit her sister Jane and her husband Bill Spence, with Henry scheduled to follow later as his duties in London allow. The Spences have two adult sons, Giles and Hamish, who effectively manage the family farm. Their most socially prominent neighbor is Sir Arthur Bratt-Cunningham, who has a daughter, Amanda. The local constable is named Denning and the vicar is Mr. Thacker. The pub is run by Paul Claverton. Simon and Bela Yately are local dog breeders.

Jane tells Emmy about Harry Heathfield, a local man who was apparently in an automobile accident in which someone was killed. Heathfield was drunk and doesn't remember anything, but is believed to have stolen the car from another customer at the pub. Jane works in animal rescue and is sent over to remove Heathfield's three dogs, but there are only two there. The newest one is missing.

Coincidentally, Henry is investigating violent tensions between two rival gangs who are involved with greyhound racing. One of the gang leaders is named Lawson, and he was the man killed in the automobile accident. Heathfield had been drinking with two men from London and the obvious early hypothesis is that they killed Lawson and framed Heathfield. Henry smells a rat when he hears the details of Lawson's death. Emmy also senses that something is wrong when the Yateleys mention that they had just given Heathfield a greyhound, since neither of the ones they rescued was that breed.

One of the London men is identified as Major Weatherby, the crooked pub manager from *Death and the Dutch Uncle*. It was Weatherby's car that was supposed to have been stolen. Thoroughly interested now, Henry goes to visit the widow and finds the house deserted. While he's there, a young man drives up claiming to be the realtor and tells Henry that the property has just been sold, but when Henry checks with the main office, they tell him that it is still for sale and that whoever he encountered was an imposter. Henry then searches the house and garden and finds evidence that a dog has been kept there recently. Back at Scotland Yard, Henry quickly identifies the fake realtor as Harry Bates, a small time crook.

Although it initially appears that there is no real mystery about what happened, Henry's investigations turn up more questions than answers. Weatherby and his companion never left the pub until after the accident so they could not have been personally involved. No one can determine how Lawson got to the countryside since his car was still back in London. And why would someone steal – and conceal – the greyhound?

The puzzle starts to unfold early on. The missing greyhound is a dead ringer for another with champion potential who is registered to the late Mr. Lawson's mother-in-law. The champion is also missing, supposedly about to give birth, but Lawson's widow refuses to say where, claiming that she had a friend of hers sell the dog. Henry learns next that Heathfield's missing dog has been entered in a race, and has won despite staggering odds and an assurance by the breeders that the dog has no competitive spirit. Clearly the champion has been substituted for the unknown dog, and probably vice versa.

This was a decided improvement over the previous two books. Although the general outline of what is happening is obvious throughout, the details are of interest in themselves, and the procedure by which Henry unravels the problem is logical and entertaining. When he gets too close to the solution he is abducted by two people, one of whom he identifies as Shorty Bates. The other never speaks and it appears that this is because Henry would recognize his or her voice. He is dumped in a shed belonging to a member of the rival gang, the same shed where at least one of the missing dogs has been held. Although nearly killed by mistake, he is rescued by the police in the nick of time.

Henry decides to let it be known that he is in critical condition and has himself smuggled out of the hospital. He and friends go to the race track where Heathfield's dog is scheduled to run next, and they find Marlene Lawson and her mother, who obviously know more than they were admitting. Weatherby shows up a few minutes later, and then Amanda Bratt-Cunningham. She clearly knows Weatherby's crooked companion by name. The companion, Albert Pennington, attempts to murder Amanda but is subdued by the police. Amanda is the one who first noticed that the two dogs were identical and told Pennington. Both gangs have now lost their leaders and the conspiracy has been ended.

Black Widower (1975) was the first of Moyes' novels to take place in the Americas, specifically Washington, D.C. Mavis Ironmonger is the rather scandalous wife of Edward Ironmonger, ambassador from the island nation of Tampica to the United States. In addition to the open rumors of her romantic affairs, Mavis is about as undiplomatic as she can be, much to the consternation of her husband and Michael Holder-Watts, the embassy's resident lawyer. The First Secretary is Winston Nelson.

They are holding a reception to celebrate the opening of the embassy and Mavis' unpredictable habits are of some concern.

Nelson is planning to leave shortly after the festivities begin to accompany retired Bishop Barrington and his wife to a dinner elsewhere. Holder-Watts has a wife, Eleanor, but despite his public contempt for Mavis, he is believed to be involved with her himself. Edward would almost certainly be prime minister if he had not been encumbered with such a notorious wife.

Various parties show up at the embassy including a group of random protesters led by Franklin Martin. Other guests include Senator George Belmont and his wife Magnolia, who are opposed to maintaining a naval base in Tampica, and Michael and Prudence Barrington, the latter of whom disapproves of Mavis quite strongly. Otis Schipmaker, a prominent businessman, is also there with his wife Virginia. Otis appears to have been one of Mavis' earlier conquests.

Despite orders to the staff not to provide Mavis with alcohol, she becomes drunk and insults one of the diplomats before being rushed off to her room where she is locked in, having passed out. Nelson and the Barringtons have seemingly already left at this point. Their daughter, Jean, has married Homer Schipmaker, Otis' older brother. Among those distressed by the scene at the embassy is Dorabella Hamilton, secretary to the ambassador, with whom she is in love.

Mavis was locked in her room at seven and her dead body is discovered there at half past eight. She died of a bullet wound to the head, which might have been self inflicted. The gun belonged to her husband but its existence was common knowledge among the embassy staff. The doctor's examination reveals that she could not possibly have been conscious when the shot was fired, so it is murder rather than suicide.

For a variety of diplomatic, political, and authorial reasons, no one wants to involve the local police so a request is placed which results in Henry Tibbett being loaned to the Tampican government to investigate. His involvement will be unofficial and will be masked by a figurehead Tampican police inspector. His visit is explained by the fact that he and Emmy are staying with old friends who live not far from the embassy.

Henry learns almost immediately that Dorabella was in love with Edward Ironmonger and hated Mavis, as did Eleanor Holder-Watts and probably Winston Nelson. Mavis had been drugged just prior to her death and the doctor saw the bottle of pills in her medicine cabinet, but they are now missing. The drug is used to treat people with alcoholism, and Holder-Watts claims that his wife was treated for it some years past, although she denies that this is true. Doralee, however, was in fact treated with the same drug that was used on Mavis.

Doralee has an appointment to meet Henry but is killed by a hit and run driver while on the way. Oddly enough, her handbag is still in her office, which causes a delay in identifying her body. Her last words include what appears to be a confession to the murder and it is possible that she threw herself in front of the car. The suspicious reader will remember that she was in love with the ambassador and might have decided to give her life for him. Henry is about to accept the suicide solution when a chance word by a near witness to the accident leads him to believe that it was murder after all.

Although he tells everyone that the case is closed, he accepts an invitation to visit Tampica. He and Emmy are surprised to discover that Otis and Virginia Schipmaker are also visiting. There is a conference underway to determine the future of an American naval base, so most of the suspects from Washington are there, as well as Mavis' parents, Mr. & Mrs. Watkins, who are visiting from England, but who prove to be just a minor distraction. Henry learns that there is a clandestine syndicate buying up land in anticipation of the naval base being closed in favor of hotel development, which he believes to be the motive in the killing, although it turns out otherwise.

This is a fair mystery that is a bit bloated at times by long descriptions of the wonders of the island. The solution to the mystery is rather obvious. Since the only people with strong alibis are the Barringtons and Nelson, Nelson is the obvious choice. This becomes even more evident when repeated mention is made of the unreliability of the bishop's watch, and later the fact that they nearly missed watching the news because the watch was so slow. This clearly points to a manipulation of the perceived time of their departure to mask Nelson's quick trip upstairs to murder Mavis, and he is eventually forced to confess.

The Coconut Killings (1977) has also appeared as *To Kill a Coconut*. The author's interest in island life continued and in fact she spent the last several years of her life in the Virgin Islands. The setting this time is another imaginary Caribbean Island, St.

Matthews, which is still British owned. The Colvilles, with whom the Tibbetts stayed while they were in Washington, have taken over a small inn on that island. They are located near a very exclusive golf club managed by Sebastian Chatsworth, whose wife is named Teresa. Everything seems very peaceful until Senator Brett Olsen is hacked to death on one of the fairways. Sanderson Robbins, a young local, has been charged.

    The arrest provokes civil unrest on the island, and a personal appeal from the Colvilles, who know Robbins and believe he is innocent. They introduce the Tibbetts to some of the islanders, including Daniel Markham, who works at the golf club, and Tom Bradley, a journalist from Washington. Olsen had come to the island with a friend, Huberman, a lobbyist, but without his wife, and he was rumored to be entertaining at least one local woman clandestinely. Huberman has brought a girlfriend, Candida Stevenson.

    Olsen and Huberman had been playing golf and Huberman appeared frantically at the clubhouse insisting that a black man with a machete had attacked them. He positively identified Robbins. Robbins admits having been there but insists that he was hired by Olsen to jump out of the underbrush with the machete in order to give Huberman a fright and that Olsen was fine when he left the scene.

    Bradley introduces Henry to Brooks and Delaware, two activists from another island who are trying to stir up trouble locally. He also meets Diamond, a young woman who is part of their organization. Diamond lost an eye because she refused sex to an unnamed member of the golf club who wanted to get even. Henry quickly ascertains that Olsen was the member in question.

    Candida lives up to her name and is quite candid. She was hired to help nudge Olsen to favor the legislative position favored by Huberman and his employers. One of those employers, Jackson Ledbetter, was on the island on the day of the murder. Candida had met Robbins and liked him, even brought him to the club bar, which had made Olsen very jealous. Rollins was at one time romantically involved with Diamond, but reportedly had broken up with her even before she lost her eye.

    Huberman and Bradley both return to the US, but Candida stays behind, now sponsored by Reynolds, an undercover policeman working for Henry. This enrages Teresa Chatsworth for reasons she refuses to explain. Then news breaks of a bribery scandal. Olsen was about to be exposed and Huberman has gone into hiding. Reynolds sends a note suggesting that Candida has been abducted but he is also missing. Meanwhile Diamond is arrested on a trumped up charge and riots ensue. This particular development is unconvincing since it is clear the charges are unsupportable and the consequences were predictable.

The rioters free both Diamond and Rollins from jail before subsiding. In the aftermath, the body of Huberman is found in one of the rooms at the golf club. He has been killed with a machete. This happened despite the fact that he is on record as having flown back to the mainland. Obviously someone took his place.

The story briefly switches to the viewpoint of Reynolds, who correctly suspects that Candida has been removed against her will. It is also obvious that someone in hotel management is working with the two hired men who have taken her. Reynolds believes that she is being held in a remote part of the island and sets out to find her. He does so, and they are promptly recaptured by the revolutionaries led by Diamond. Henry accompanies the rescue party and Reynolds and company are freed. Diamond and her friends get away, but only after they kill Ledbetter, who was responsible for the deaths of Huberman and Olsen.

This isn't a bad story although it feels skeletal. Events happen too quickly for the reader to properly digest them and since the general outline of what has happened is quite obvious, the mystery itself is less enticing. The revolutionary group never seems even remotely plausible and that entire portion of the plot requires a considerable suspension of disbelief. The late introduction of a new motive – the possibility of the island opening cotton plantations that would adversely affect mainland commerce – is a rather blatant instance of cheating the reader by withholding information, and is any case of doubtful relevance since the government intended to develop tourism, not agriculture.

Who Is Simon Warwick? (1979) makes use of one of the classic mystery conventions - the question of identifying the correct heir to a fortune. This device is largely obsolete now since DNA testing would eliminate the need for deductive analysis. Attorney Ambrose Quince is executor of the will of Lord Charlton which leaves his estate to the son of a disgraced brother. The son was adopted by a couple who moved to the US and Lord Charlton has never met his new beneficiary, who was originally named Simon Warwick. His new identity is, of course, unknown.

Lord Charlton was already dying when the will was written so it is no surprise that no claimants turn up until shortly after his death. The first is Harold Benson from Virginia. He claims that his adopted parents – who are now both deceased – managed to get a new but false birth certificate in his new name. He has what appears to be the original passport made out for Simon Warwick as an infant. A few days later Simon Finch appears, making the same claim, and he has correspondence from the lawyer – now deceased – who handled the adoption. This suggests that he is in fact Simon Warwick. Finch claims to have been attending school in England during which period he ran away and has not communicated with his adopted parents since.

Quince and his wife travel to Virginia where they are unable to either confirm or deny Benson's story. Suggestively, Benson's wife leaves town despite an appointment, claiming that her son is ill, but Quince discovers almost immediately that she was lying to avoid the meeting. Although he cannot find incontrovertible evidence, Quince concludes that Finch is Warwick and decides to proceed with the settlement of the estate.

Quince and his partner, Bertram Hamstone, announce their intentions at a dinner party whose guests consist of Cecily Smeed, who was Lord Charlton's personal secretary, Denton Westbury, and Sir Percy Crumble and his wife Diana. In the event that Simon Warwick is not found and settled with the estate, the previous will goes into force, which included a substantial sum for Smeed, so she is understandably unhappy. Sir Percy manages Charlton's business interests and has had a free hand for many years, which would not be the case if Simon Warwick became majority stockholder. Westbury was to have administered the distribution of the substantial estate among various charities and will therefore be out of a job.

Quince invites both claimants to meet at his office at ten, but Finch shows up half an hour early, saying that he received a message altering the time. The secretary shows him into the waiting room. Half an hour later Benson arrives and is sent into the same room, but he immediately returns saying that there is a dead man inside. Finch has been strangled.

A Mrs. Goodman turns up a short while later and insists that she recognizes the picture of Simon Finch and that he is her son, Ronald Goodman, and clearly not Simon Warwick. He worked for the law firm that handled the adoption, so that explains his access to the papers he carried, and proves clearly that he was an imposter. This suggests that Benson really is Simon Warwick, unless he too is a criminal, and Henry believes that might well be the case. Henry also learns that Smeed and Westbury are long time friends.

It has been obvious from early on that the baby had some identifying physical feature because Lord Charlton was quite certain he would be able to identify the real heir if he lived long enough to actually meet him, which he did not. We have subsequently learned that the baby was delivered to his new parents by Diana Crumble, so it is reasonable to assume that she would recognize him also, but by a very late point in the book Henry has still not talked to her. Henry also believes that the real Simon Warwick has yet to come forward, but that he is aware of what has been going on and may in fact be the murderer. The fact that Westbury turns out to be an assumed name is suggestive but not convincing, since he knew Lord Charlton and had not been recognized.

Benson insists that someone tried to push him under a bus. Henry arrests him and charges him with murder, even though he is not convinced that he has the right person. When Benson hears that his wife is flying to England to be with him, he is clearly in a panic and given Henry's earlier suspicions, it is surprising that he does not suspect that this is not the real Harold Benson and that the wife will realize that immediately if she sees him. The distinguished mark turns out to be mismatched eye coloring.

Emmy decides to meet Mrs. Benson at the airport but she is whisked away in a hired car the moment she arrives. Emmy does notice that her eyes are different colors and the pieces fall into place. Simon Warwick has had a sex change operation. Through luck, Emmy gets herself invited to share the car and they are taken to a rendezvous with another vehicle, driven by a third woman. She disappears, turns up, then disappears again and is finally menaced by Ambrose, the lawyer, whose activities late in the book have become increasingly suspicious.

This is certainly the best of her later mysteries. There are layers of deceit so that the solution of one puzzle reveals another and the insertion of red herrings is effective and dramatically appropriate. The fact that the real motive is not revealed until very late is a mild cheat, but it could be presumed from the facts at hand.

Angel Death (1980) takes the Tibbetts to the fictional island of St Marks in the Caribbean. It opens with the mysterious disappearance of a small yacht along with its two passengers. Henry and Emmy Tibbett are about to return to the area, on vacation this time. They are staying at the inn owned by their friends the Colvilles, along with Betsy Sprague, who knew the woman lost on the yacht, Janet Vanduren. Shortly after she tells the Tibbetts about her last meeting with Janet, she calls from the harbor and tells them that she has just seen Janet and is going to go after her. Not surprisingly, no one ever sees her again.

Emmy insists on trying to find the missing woman and Henry reluctantly goes along, although his own curiosity is whetted when they find a souvenir that Sprague had bought in the shallow water next to one of the piers. The local authorities are only as cooperative as they need to be, convinced that there is nothing amiss. They trace the missing woman to another yacht, but that one also disappears at sea. Since there has been considerable talk of the drug smuggling in the background – Moyes had an exaggerated idea of the dangers of marijuana – it's fairly obvious that the disappearances are connected.

The local police explain that the drug traffic is so lucrative that it is general practice to sink each yacht after one delivery. They assume that Vanduren is actively involved, that she lured Sprague aboard and disposed of her body at sea, and then probably switched to another boat. Vanduren's mother has supposedly had a nervous breakdown and her father is obstructive, suggesting he may have been aware of her involvement in the drug trade or even a participant. This turns out to be a partial red herring.

Henry proceeds to get involved with a rowdy crowd and leaves Emmy. This is transparently an attempt to go undercover and it should have been as obvious to the villains as it is to the reader. He is drugged by the gang – not very convincingly – and eventually finds himself wanted by the police after he behaves disgracefully in his drug induced stupor. This gives Moyes the opportunity to tell a good deal of the story from Emmy's point of view, but unfortunately Moyes did not really develop her character and Henry's exploits are unconvincing.

This was a dramatically disappointing novel, more adventure than mystery, but with too laconic a story line to succeed in that format. There is almost no mystery involved and some of the details are explained tediously and unnecessarily. The resolution depends heavily on coincidence, including a vague reference to a picnic which a radio operator recounts to Henry, who recognizes it as a code. This was by far her weakest novel.

A Six-Letter Word for Death (1983) has a clever opening. Someone sends Henry Tibbett a blank crossword puzzle and then, over a period of time, sets of clues. He consults the eccentric but brilliant Bishop Manciple whom we met in *Murder Fantastical* and they solve the puzzle, which refers to three separate and apparently unrelated deaths, all of which were deemed to be of natural causes, but all of which also resulted in substantial inheritances. Henry believes that the puzzle was sent to him as a practical joke by the members of the Guess Who club, a group of pseudonymous murder mystery writers whom he is to address on the Isle of Wight. The clues in the puzzle also reveal the secret identities of all of the writers in the Guess Who club. This proves to be correct as it turns out that one of the writers is Henry Vandike, who does expert crossword puzzles under his own name.

Other members of the club include Fred Coe, an economist, Dr. William Cartwright, Myrtle Waterford, and Barbara Oppenshaw, daughter of the owner of the firm that publishes all of the members' books. Barbara's father Robert is sponsoring the week long get together. Others in the house include Barbara's stepmother, Pamela, and her fiancé, Peter Turnberry.

Most of the crossword clues were connected to the names of the participants and potentially suspicious deaths in their past. One mentions Eugenia Warfield, who supposedly died by drowning some twenty years earlier. Eugenia was the stepdaughter of Pamela Oppenshaw by a previous marriage. Eugenia's death was declared accidental, but she had multiple sclerosis and might have been aware that she did not have long to live. Henry reveals the solution to the puzzle and everything seems to have a benevolent explanation, but Turnberry quietly asks Henry to meet with him later.

The various guests disperse on individual business that afternoon and Turnberry borrows a horse to ride over to his parents' home which is nearby. He is there only a few minutes to collect something, the nature of which is unknown. When he doesn't return for his appointment, Barbara expresses concern, but also admits that she had called off their engagement the night before, convinced that Peter was a fortune hunter.

The man who runs the stable tells Henry that something is wrong. The horse returns without its saddle, and he insists that the girth could not have broken. He also doesn't understand why it took so long for the horse to return since it certainly knew its way. Turnberry's body is found at the foot of a cliff but there are certain abnormalities. There are no marks on his hands suggesting he tried to arrest his slide down from the trail to the precipice. Henry finds the saddle and suspects the girth has been cut, also noting that it was lying away from the cliff and almost hidden. Whatever Turnberry had retrieved from his home is missing and a piece of rope is tied to a nearby tree, suggesting that the horse was tethered there but broke free. When someone moves the saddle again before the search party arrives, Henry knows that it was murder.

Henry and Emmy decide not to return to London right away. They visit the Turnberry family, from whom they learn that their son had been close friends with Vandike, whom he knew from college. Barbara Oppenshaw tells Henry that she had recently discovered that Turnberry had been after her parents' money and that is why she was not devastated by his death.

Belatedly, Henry decides to ask Vandike about the inclusion of some clues that have not been explained, most obviously the connection between Peter Turnberry and keys. This is a mild flaw since this is such an obvious and compelling part of the solution that it should have been investigated immediately. By then Vandike has gone off mountain climbing and is unreachable. Henry also refrains from bringing up any of the contrary evidence at the inquest, as does the local police constable, to whom he had confided the truth. While this is somewhat plausible given Henry's belief that he can better trap the criminal by deception, there is no explanation of why the local officer would suppress the truth, despite being under no pressure from Henry to do so, unless someone else – the Oppenshaws – were applying it.

Henry gets Cartwright to admit that he took his car out around the time Turnberry was killed, and the explanation is an obvious lie. Myrtle Waterford rather hostilely claims that Turnberry came to her with a story idea that she rejected, and she denies claims that Oppenshaw had declined to publish any more of her books out of fear that she was plagiarizing American authors. Coe confirms that Turnberry was shopping around a mystery plot during the get together. The plot was clearly related to the accidental drowning that occurred when Barbara was six.

Although the Oppenshaws have what appears to be an ironclad alibi for the time of Turnberry's death, it turns out that they have an excellent motive for having wanted the stepdaughter dead. Pamela is the one who inherited the money and property, but it was only supposed to be for her lifetime or until she married, after which it would have gone to the stepdaughter. When Eugenia died, Pamela became the sole legatee. The solution begins to unfold when we learn two things. First, the will designated that Eugenia's children, if any, would inherit if she died, and Eugenia was eighteen when she drowned. Second, Peter Turnberry was adopted and the adoption was arranged by Vandike. Cartwright was also aware of the fact that Turnberry was adopted.

Vandike then appears to have disappeared while mountain climbing, but the day he supposedly vanished he was actually in London having lunch with Henry. The staff at the club where they ate have, however, been bribed into denying that he was present. Henry concludes that it was meant to be another practical joke, but that the murderer had taken advantage of the confusion to eliminate Vandike, who knew too much of the truth.

The ultimate solution includes a quite nicely done reversal. According to Henry, Peter was not the illegitimate son of Eugenia and heir to the estate. Vandike was simply constructing another elaborate and cruel practical joke by leading him to believe that that was the case. Henry tells the assembled suspects that he believes Vandike accosted Peter to prevent him from showing the fake adoption papers to anyone and that Peter was probably killed accidentally. After that, Vandike returned to his mountain climbing and may have fallen to his own death some time later. Emmy, however, knows that this is not the true story.

The truth is that Peter WAS in fact Eugenia's son, and that Cartwright was the father. Since she was a minor at the time, the Oppenshaws had blackmailed him into getting Barbara out of the way while Eugenia was being murdered, and later manipulated him in their attempt to kill Vandike, who turns out to be alive after all, having cleverly faked his own death. Pamela killed Peter and she and her husband unsuccessfully tried to murder Vandike.

This is one of Moyes' better novels, patterned after classic detective stories with complicated and arcane clues, a gathering of the suspects, an eccentric will, and hidden identities. Some of the solution requires extraordinary intuition on Henry's part, but not enough to invalidate the logic that brings him to trap the real killers. The ironclad alibi is a mild cheat because the reader is never told that it was not in fact all that difficult to leave a party unobserved.

The Tibbetts are returning from yet another vacation -, this time in the Netherlands to visit characters met in *Murder and the Dutch Uncle* - at the opening of *Night Ferry to Death* (1985). While they are there, a major jewel theft takes place in Amsterdam. To return to England, they board the night ferry of the title, but all of the cabins have been booked by a business delegation so Henry and Emmy and several others, including a rude and obviously frightened man who loudly insisted that he required a cabin, are forced to resort to sleeping chairs in a large lounge. In the morning, they discover that the rude man has been stabbed to death. The other passengers in the lounge include Erica van der Molen, an English woman married to a Dutch husband who is not aboard, and her young daughter Susan. None of the others are identified at this point.

Upon arriving in England, the ferry is met by Inspector Harris, who tells Henry that the dead man was a known thief believed to be carrying the diamonds stolen in the Dutch jewel robbery. They hoped to follow him to the mastermind behind the crime, but now they have no leads, and no diamonds. The lounge door was not locked at night so initially it seems possible that even those passengers who had cabins could be potential suspects. One of the crewmen eventually insists that he had the door in sight all night and that no one entered or left, so they are eliminated.

Since it is not Henry's case, he returns to London, only to discover that he is being assigned to head the investigation. He learns that another of the passengers was Solomon Rosenberg, a successful diamond dealer, which automatically makes him a prime suspect. About the same time Emmy surprises an intruder in their house who escapes unseen. When a second attempt is also thwarted, it is obvious that they are being targeted directly, presumably by someone who thinks they have the diamonds, perhaps unwittingly. The fact that the burglar is interested primarily in the bathroom suggests a connection to an incident aboard the ferry, when Emmy gave her travel kit to Susan van der Molen. The reader is certain to assume at this point that the dead man concealed the diamonds among Emmy's things, possibly planning to retrieve them later. But how was this information passed on to whoever is looking for them now? That explanation seems unlikely at first, but then Moyes pulls the rug out from under our feet, because Emmy finds the diamonds concealed within other items from their trip.

The situation suggests that there were two people involved, one who stole the jewels from the dead man, the other the one who killed him. The jewels were probably placed in Emmy's travel bag to divert suspicion from the thief, who did not want to be accused of murder, and the circumstances suggest that Erica van der Molen might have concealed them during their encounter. Since the police did not search her travel bag before it left the ferry – the Tibbetts were considered above suspicion - the thief realized there was a chance to recover them before they were discovered. Another likely suspect is Margaret Hartford-Brown, the English woman who was also in the washroom where the travel bag was unattended.

The third burglary attempt was anticipated and the man involved is captured by the police, but he is a small time crook and very uncooperative, obviously hired for this specific job and not privy to the information the police are looking for. In fact, Henry believes he was meant to be caught so that the police would stop watching the house. Sure enough, a woman pretending to be a friend of Jane's sister visits and steals the bag of pebbles which has been substituted for the diamonds. Emmy recognizes her as being one of the people in the ferry lounge but pretends not to have noticed, since she knows the police will follow her when she leaves.

Based on the reports from the search, the woman is either named Watson or Spencer. The policewoman following her sees her write and mail a letter, then go into a restroom where she fatally shoots herself, presumably having discovered that she does not have the diamonds after all. Both Watson and Spencer are away from home, so it is uncertain which of them is dead, but it turns out that Watson had claimed that Margaret's husband was her brother. Margaret is back in the Netherlands, but Henry interviews her story is presented makes this unlikely as it would be too obvious. In fact the most likely explanation is that it was designed to put the inn out of business, which would directly benefit Pargeter, who was not present.

The first person format enables Moyes to skip the routine interviews with the kitchen staff, which confirms that they are not to be taken as serious suspects. If one of them was involved, the reader would have been privy to their direct testimony. Unfortunately later this results in Henry inviting Susan to attend more critical interviews so that she can tell the reader, and this situation does not ring true at all.

James comes and goes and there are some little signs of a concealed, unpleasant personality. He proposes and Susan tells him that she doesn't love him, which is in itself a flashing warning sign to the reader that something is wrong with him, although she later convinces herself that she is wrong. Some members of the Manciple family from *Death and the Dutch Uncle* make brief appearances. Emmy accompanies Henry, but this time she contributes very little to the story. Nor is Henry a shining light of detection. He arrests the heir and the waiter and charges them with murder on what appears to be no real evidence at all and without an explanation of how they could have known what the victim was going to order for dinner. Not surprisingly, a second diner is fatally poisoned some time later while both men are in prison.

There are hints that Pargeter may have been involved in the death of Susan's aunt, who drowned in the river near the inn, and who may have been murdered by her husband. His personal fortune has also disappeared over the years, and one explanation might be blackmail, possibly by Pargeter. There are a few red herrings but they are more after thoughts than actual plot elements. It is quite obvious that James is not going to be Susan's romantic interest – although they do eventually get married, nor is he an acknowledged suspect, so the only reason why the author would have included him among the characters was because he is the murderer.

The first part of the solution involves a very fortunate coincidence, after which Susan does some detecting herself when Pargeter gives a totally inadequate explanation about why he would like to visit her wine cellar. It is clear that he was after the photographs that had been used to blackmail her uncle, who almost certainly did murder his wife. Susan has already found them and turned them over to Henry.

Against her better judgment, Susan has married James, after which an attempt is made on her life. A second attempt provides the climax after which Henry explains all. The motive – a possible factory site which would raise local property values – is not revealed until the end, which is really not fair to the reader. There are also some very contrived scenes designed to throw suspicion on other characters at the last minute that are not remotely convincing.

Overall, Moyes was one of more entertaining stories of light detection. Her strengths were primarily in characterization and puzzle construction. The occasional foray into more overt action – particularly the Caribbean novels – rarely proved as successful. Her attempt to include Emmy as an active part of the investigation varied from slight to intensive, but sometimes required that Henry act in very unprofessional ways in order to accommodate her inclusion. She was much better at third person narration and sometimes encountered structural difficulties with first person which were not smoothly handled. Her best novel was *Murder Fantastical*, but her best mystery may have been *Who Is Simon Warwick?*

EARL DERR BIGGERS

Earl Derr Biggers (1884-1933) was a novelist and playwright who is best known for his six Charlie Chan novels, which inspired a long series of inferior movies. His first mystery novel was *Seven Keys to Baldpate* (1913), which was adapted for the stage and filmed in 1917. The play resulted in several movies and the novel was used for two more, *House of the Long Shadows* and *Haunted Honeymoon*.

Except for some incidental scenes, the novel has only two sets, a hotel room and a lobby. William Magee is a writer who has traveled to a remote town en route to a refuge in which to finish his novel. Upon his arrival he encounters a young woman crying at the station, but she politely refuses his help and goes off with her mother. He is looking for Elijah Quimby, caretaker of Baldpate Inn, a resort which is currently closed for the season, having arranged to be allowed to stay there despite the lack of heat and electricity in order to have peace and quiet while he works. But within hours of his having moved in, he discovers a young man who identifies himself as Joseph Bland in the lobby. Bland, who carries a revolver, quickly locks something in the safe before pretending to be sociable.

Bland provides an entirely unconvincing reason for his presence and pressures Magee to leave. Magee invents a fictional reason of his own and insists that he is going to stay. Bland settles down in another room but before either of them can go to sleep there is the sound of a gunshot and breaking glass from the ground floor. Bland announces that he fired at someone who was trying to force the front door. The mystery man is Professor Thaddeus Bolton, who reveals that he also has a key, bringing the total to three. Bolton claims to be hiding out from reporters after he made an injudicious public statement about suffragettes. Magee then offers Bland's story as his own, so Bland is forced to employ Magee's fictional explanation, but the two men clearly are wary of one another.

The following morning another stranger shows up. Jake Peters claims to be a local recluse. He carries the morning paper which contains two stories that attract Magee's attention. One concerns a bank cashier who embezzled a great deal of money and whose description matches Bland, and the other tells of a college instructor found dead and an older professor from the same institution who is missing. His two companions counter with another story from the paper about an art thief who bears some resemblance to Magee himself. Their conversation is then interrupted by the arrival of the woman from the station, Mary Norton, and her mother. She claims to be an actress who has dropped out of sight for publicity reasons, but she admits privately to Magee that her story is a lie.

The following morning does little to clear the confusion. Mary Norton tells Magee that she believes he is one of three opposing forces gathered in the Inn despite his honest denial. He also hears the story of a man who disappeared from the Inn a few years earlier, and there are hints that Quimby may have a long standing grudge because of the suppression of a safety device he invented. The next arrival is Mayor Cargan and his repulsive aide, Lou Max. They have the fifth key. Some of the fog of mystery lifts as we discover that the focus of everything is whatever Bland locked in the Inn's safe, a safe to which none of them have the combination. But the arrangements appear to have been made by the recently fired manager of the Inn, who still had access to at least one of the seven existing keys.

Norton tells Magee that the object in the safe is a bundle of money and he agrees to try to secure it for her. There is a falling out among the conspirators when the combination is not provided on time by the absent manager, so the mayor and his friend subdue Bland, break open the safe, and secure the package. They are then attacked by a stranger and in the confusion Magee comes away with the money, only to be accosted by another new arrival, Myra Thornhill, who also implores him to help her secure the prize. Uncertain of what he should do, Magee hides the money, but it is found by the Professor, who is then attacked and robbed by Bland. The musical chairs with the package of money continues when he hides it in the kitchen, where it is found by the hermit, but then taken away by the Professor again. Meanwhile, the man who originally planned the money to be a payoff to the Mayor, Hayden, has arrived and announces that he has decided not to pay him after all.

There is a free for all when the money turns up again and the mysterious unidentified figure is named at last. Hayden identifies him as Kendrick, a man whom he thought was dead, and then suddenly kills himself without explanation. Six years earlier he had conned Kendrick into leaving the country, leaving his fiancé –

Thornhill – in the dark. Kendrick spent years believing that the police were going to arrest him. Magee gives the money to Mary Norton and holds everyone else at gunpoint until she makes her escape. The Professor and Kendrick reveal that they were working for the city prosecutor and were trying to get the money as evidence against Cargan. Despite everyone's frustration, they all leave the Inn in good humor – even Magee and the hermit. Norton turns out to be a newspaper reporter who breaks the story and presumably ends Cargan's spree of corruption.

It is not surprising that this was adapted as a popular play. The settings are very limited and the characters come and go in a fashion very similar to actors on a stage. The dialogue is crisp and witty and while the mystery is actually somewhat convoluted, it unfolds in a linear and quite accessible fashion. Although it is a mystery, it is not about a murder. The plot is a carefully choreographed dance among the characters, none of whom except for Hayden – who only appears briefly – are actually bad people. Even the corrupt mayor and his flunky are described by their enemies as admirable, even noble.

The Agony Column, filmed as *Second Floor Mystery* in 1930, is a novella first published in 1916. Geoffrey West, an American, is in England during the buildup to World War I. The title refers to the Personals column in a British newspaper. A fleeting encounter with an American tourist and her father leads him to place a clever listing of his own. She is amused and responds that he may write her seven letters, after which she will decide whether or not to speak to him in person. In the first letter, West describes how he came to be living in a house nearby, directly beneath the rooms occupied by a British military officer

His story is quite unusual. He was visiting Germany when he made the acquaintance of an English tourist who seemed to take a liking to him. When it came time for him to move on to England, his new friend gave him a letter of introduction to his cousin, Captain Fraser-Freer, who is now his neighbor. But when he presents the letter, the captain informs him that he has no such cousin. West has read the letter, which is quite lengthy, but it seemed to convey no special meaning. He is understandably embarrassed.

The next night, West hears a fight in the room above him. He goes to investigate and is nearly run into by a heavy set man who flees precipitately. The captain has been stabbed to death, and on his desk are a scarab pin and a homburg, along with four daily newspapers, all folded open to the agony column. West checks his own copies, finds references to the pin and the hat, concludes that the entries were a clandestine means of communication, and conveys this information to the police, who are already suspicious of his involvement.

The plot thickens. A mysterious woman appears in West's room, holds him at gunpoint, and orders him to lie to the police about the time of the attack or they will receive the phony letter of recommendation, which she insists will result in his imprisonment. Then the dead man's brother and father show up and ask him to do the same so that the brother can plead guilty to the murder to preserve the family honor, although he will not explain what sin the dead man committed. Then a colonel who has befriended West and who clearly knows more than he is revealing suggests that he do the same thing, promising him that the brother will be exonerated.

West tells the lie and the brother is arrested, but then the colonel appears with the gun toting woman, who also confesses to the crime, insisting it was a lovers' quarrel that got out of hand. The solution is surprising, but it cheats a great deal. The captain was trying to entice a master spy into revealing his identity and was killed for his pains. The colonel discovers by means of a fingerprint – of which the reader knows nothing – that the fingerprint is that of the police inspector assigned to the case. Revealed as the master spy, he kills himself and the case is solved. Or is it? In his final letter West reveals that he invented the entire story, based on some odd entries in the agony column, just to hold her attention. The story is amusing and clever and rather original.

Fifty Candles (1921), another novella, filmed that same year, opens with a Chinese American attempting to return to the US after his political efforts in China put him in jeopardy of his life. Due to the intimidation of other Chinese Americans who would otherwise have supported his claim to citizenship, he is denied re-entry. The story then leaps forward twenty years and is narrated by a businessman named Winthrop who was cheated by his employer an who has just returned to the US after an unsuccessful shipboard romance. He perhaps unwisely accepts an invitation to the birthday party of the man who wronged him, Drew, solely because the woman he tried to woo, Mary Will, is attending. Also present is

Drew's wife Carlotta, who is notorious for cheating on him, an enigmatic Chinese servant, and Parker, the ship's doctor and one of her conquests. There is also an estranged son, who does not appear to be present at the crucial time.

Predictably, Drew is murdered. Winthrop chases a shadowy figure, gets lost in the maze of streets, encounters Parker who also claims to be have become disoriented, and the two bring the police back to the house. There is a clumsy sequence in which we are told that Will hid the murder weapon, a knife, because she briefly believed that Winthrop was responsible and wanted to protect him. But it seems unlikely that she would have known that the knife belonged to him. Winthrop also contends that Parker stole the knife from his luggage while they were still aboard the ship, which also seem improbable given the fact that there was no way of knowing that Drew would invite them both to the party.

Drew's business partner is summoned and is found similarly stabbed to death. The ending is a bit rushed and it is badly telegraphed. Obviously the Chinese servant is the man who was to have been extradited twenty years earlier. In exchange for being allowed to switch identities, he promised twenty years of service and the fifty candles were for HIS birthday, which was evident since there was no one else in that age range. He wanted revenge against the two evil men who ruined his life, and he also was in love with the partner's wife, whom we don't know about until the climax. Rather than go to jail, he commits suicide.

Biggers clearly had a formula for his stories. The wise cracking protagonist is always pressing his suit with an often reluctant young woman. He is also suspected by the police for a significant portion of the story although we know that he is innocent. Anticipating the Charlie Chan books, Biggers treats his Chinese characters with dignity and respect. They don't talk pigeon English and they are just as likely to be intelligent and courageous as the Occidental characters.

The Dollar Chasers (1924) was his third novella. A young reporter is assigned to interview a businessman recently returned from Asia. He is one of the guests on a yacht owned by Jim Batchelor, another successful businessman whose daughter has attracted the reporter's eye. Batchelor is very superstitious, particularly about the silver dollar he always carries with him. When the lucky coin is stolen, the reporter decides to find out took it in order to ingratiate himself with his intended father-in-law. A series or revelations reveal that the coin was stolen from the original thief, and possibly then stolen again. Although less impressive than the previous two novellas, this is still a first class story and it is unfortunate that it is largely unknown today.

Although this appears to be a break from his usual pattern, it really isn't. Although the young woman in this case welcomes the protagonist's suit, her father is not disposed to allow a poor man into the family, and this reservation serves the same dramatic purpose. And while he is never seriously suspected of being responsible for the theft, his insistence that he can solve the case – followed by his failure – tarnishes his reputation in the same fashion as the false accusations in the other two novellas.

Charlie Chan of the Honolulu police force made his first appearance in *The House Without a Key* (1926), which was first filmed in 1926 and then remade in 1933 as Charlie *Chan's Greatest Case*. Amos and Daniel Winterslip are brothers who live on adjacent plots of land in Hawaii, but they have not spoken in more than thirty years. Dan, the rich one, is hosting Minerva Winterslip, their cousin, who has been on an extended stay in the islands. His daughter Barbara has recently returned from college and another cousin, John Quincy Winterslip, Minerva's nephew, is also en route to Hawaii, ostensibly on vacation, actually this is intended as a goad to bring Minerva home to Boston. Dan has recently been involved romantically with Arlene Compton, whose reputation is nuanced. He has also reputedly not been entirely above board in his business dealings, and the air of mystery is initiated when he takes an inordinate interest in the arrival of John Quincy.

John is the protagonist, a somewhat stuffy but basically good hearted man who has a brief encounter with a young woman while in San Francisco. The two of them make up the inevitable pairing found in all of Biggers' mysteries. Dan sends a letter to John in San Francisco requesting that he visit the former's mainland house, secure a locked box, and dispose of it. Puzzled, he attempts to comply but he is attacked inside the house and the box is missing when he recovers. Then he meets Barbara, who is sailing to Hawaii on the same ship, along with her friend Harry Jennison, who happens to be Dan's lawyer. During the voyage, John meets an elderly missionary who recounts meeting Dan Winterslip when he was a young man, and credits himself with having convinced Dan to give up the slave trade.

Just before the boat docks in Hawaii, Minerva returns from a late night party to find an unknown intruder in the house – he or she escapes unidentified – and Dan stabbed to death. She calls Amos, who calls the police, and Charlie Chan arrives with another detective and a doctor. They quickly ascertain that the dead man has an appointment to meet with Jim Egan, a local hotel manager, at eleven that evening, and that he died at about quarter past one. One of the servants reports hearing raised voices at ten, a woman and two men – one of whom was the victim – but she cannot identify the other two. A page has been torn from a guest book which listed all the visitors Dan had entertained.

Most of the initial interrogation is handled by Captain Hallett, with Charlie Chan in the background. Biggers deliberately chose a low key profile for Chan, both as a method of lulling the reader, as well as the various characters, into underestimating his abilities. This technique is replicated noticeably in the Columbo television series, and for much the same purposes. Charlie is Chinese and speaks English quite well, although usually in short or incomplete sentences. He is also quite heavy and unlikely to be pursuing criminals in foot races or wrestling weapons from their grasp.

This initial setup divides the characters into two sets, one potentially associated with each of the crimes. Since the ship from San Francisco has not yet docked, John, Barbara, Jennison, a steward named Bowker, and the missionary are apparently not viable candidates for the murder, but one of them may have assaulted John and stolen the mystery box. There is also a military officer, Captain Cope, who may have traveled on an earlier vessel and therefore in theory could have committed the assault and the murder. Minerva, Egan, Amos, two servants, and Arlene Compton are on the island and therefore suspect, although we see Minerva's return to the house through her eyes and she is clearly not guilty. One might normally eliminate the servants, but Biggers picked one as the killer in *Fifty Candles*, so that would be premature. It is evident that something from the dead man's past had resurfaced, something linked to the purloined box, although this was not necessarily the cause of his murder.

One of the servants comes to Minerva with a piece of jewelry which she says that Dan gave to Compton some time back. She found it near the body but did not inform the police. She prevails upon John to accompany the police and keep the family in the loop. Their first visit is to Egan, who admits that he once met Dan years earlier but hadn't spoken to him again until the night of the murder, and he refuses outright to explain what business the two men had together. We finally learn the identity of the woman John met in San Francisco; she is Egan' daughter, Carlota. Egan insists that he came and went by the front door, but one of the distinctive cigarettes that he smokes was found outside the other entrance, near the body.

John learns of the lost jewelry and confronts Mrs. Compton, and in the process meets her "friend", Leatherbee. She insists that she did not visit Dan but that he came to see her, insisting that she return the jewelry for unspecified reasons. She later admits to the police that she and Leatherbee accompanied him back to his own house briefly and they were obviously the ones who argued with him. One more character needs to be mentioned. Mr. Saladine appears to be comic relief – he lost his false teeth while swimming – but the multiple reference to him suggest that he has a greater role to play, particularly when he is caught at one point eavesdropping on a police interrogation.

Carlota tells John that she found a check for five thousand dollars made out to her father and signed by Dan, which suggests blackmail, although it seems to them that it is strong evidence vindicating her father, who is in police custody for withholding information. That same evening the police prevent Leatherbee from boarding a boat to leave the islands and in his possession is the missing page from the guestbook. The missing entry refers to someone named John Gleason and Leatherbee claims that Dan gave him the page and told him to look Gleason up when he reached Australia. If he is telling the truth, this is a good example of the false clue, a red herring designed to keep the reader guessing about how all the separate parts fit into the puzzle.

Chan tracks down the contents of a fragment of newspaper that Dan tore off hastily the night of his death. It refers to the arrival in Honolulu of Thomas Brade, which is the name of the supposedly deceased captain of the slave vessel on which he once served as first mate. Brade's initials were also on the stolen box. The disparate pieces are slowly being drawn together. Brade, who also smokes the obscure brand of cigarette found at the murder scene – as does Captain Cope - has been missing from his hotel for several days.

Events start to build for the climax when the grandson of one of Dan's servants shows up at the hotel with a package for Brade, a package which contains the stolen but still locked box. The box is empty but when Brade is eventually located – he is the son of the captain of the slave ship - he explains that Dan stole the man's considerable store of cash and jewels when he died, and that he was planning to pay for the empty box as evidence in a lawsuit. The distinctive piece of jewelry is also mentioned in a surviving letter, which explains the desperate effort to recover it from Compton. Brade, however, is unlikely to have murdered the man whom he hoped to confront in court. The grandson, however, admits to having talked a friend into stealing the box, and is then identified as having been near the Winterslip house at approximately the time of the murder.

There is a hint of the modern police procedural at this point Chan reveals that the cigarette in question comes in two blends. A consultation with an expert reveals that the incriminating stub matches that smoked by Cope, but not those in the possession of Egan or Brade. This changes the focus of suspicion, but that shift is complicated by the revelation that Cope is Jim Egan's older brother and by an attempt on John's life, bullets fired at him by an unknown assailant while he is touring the island with Carlota after having negotiated a settlement for Brade for the crime committed against his family. Egan admits to having blackmailed Dan, but insists that he would never have actually cashed the check.

The police now only possess two unexplained clues. One is a button believed to have been dropped by the killer. The other is the fact that when Minerva briefly saw him, she recognized a distinctive watch face that glowed in the dark. But just as they are running out of lines of inquiry, they discover that Saladine is a false identity. Unfortunately, Chan's superior tells them to forget Saladine, suggesting correctly that he is an undercover policeman.

John is then assaulted and abducted by three men but manages to get free. One of his assailants wears a watch with the distinct flaw Minerva spotted on the night of the murder. Its current owner is identified – a taxi driver – but it clearly was not his until recently.

Chan traces it back to a man named Cabrera, a friend of the steward, Bowker. Then he and John, following different chains of reasoning, figure out who the killer is.

Although the solution is satisfactory, it involves considerable cheating in the form of withheld information. We are not told until the end that it would be possible to leave the anchored ship and swim to shore and back leaving enough time to kill Dan. Nor do we know that Chan observed bribe money being passed to Bowker or that Cabrera worked for Jennison, who killed to prevent a change in the dead man's will that would have disinherited his daughter if she had married him. A detective novel should always ensure that the reader and the detective have access to the same information, although they may differently measure its significance.

The structure of the novel is quite complex, although Biggers was skillful enough to present a rather large cast of characters and motives in such a logical fashion that the reader will be mystified but never confused. Unlike many mystery novelists who store up nearly all the revelations for the final scenes, he allows Chan and even other characters to solve subsidiary puzzles along the way. He is more traditional in his choice of narrator, wisely avoiding telling things from Chan's point of view since this would necessarily reveal too much too soon. John Winterslip functions as a kind of Doctor Watson, contributing slightly but present largely as an external viewpoint capable of chronicling the process of discovery rather than the actual events.

The Chinese Parrot (1926) – filmed in 1927 and remade as *Charlie Chan's Courage* in 1934 - opens with Sally Jordan trying to arrange for the sale of her pearls. Her husband died years earlier leaving her son Victor to run the business, and he made a mess of it, placing the family on the verge of bankruptcy. The prospective buyer is P.J. Madden, who wants them for his daughter Evelyn. His personal secretary is Martin Thorn. The agent for the transaction is a jeweler named Alexander Eden whose own son, Robert, is considering a career as a reporter. The sale takes place in San Francisco and the pearls are to be brought over from Hawaii by Charlie Chan. Bob Eden is assigned to meet him but when he arrives the young man is missing. Madden had insisted that they be delivered to him in New York, but Eden receives a call purporting to be from him and changing the rendezvous to his ranch in the

Southwest. West prudently calls Madden back for confirmation and is told the same thing again, but readers will be pardonably skeptical. Biggers would not have taken such pains with the diverging sets of plans if they were not significant.

There is a whopping coincidence early on. Charlie visits a relative in San Francisco, whose daughter happens to be a switchboard operator, who happened to process a call from Chinatown to Madden's ranch, and happens to recall the message – that the ranch manager, Louis Wong, should come to San Francisco as soon as possible. Bob Eden did not meet Chan because he realized that he was being followed by at least one and possibly two individuals whose looks he distrusted. One of these men is identified as Phil Maydorf, a known criminal, and Chan spots him at the establishment where the call to the ranch originated. He recognizes that they are heading into some sort of trap.

Eden and Chan travel to the Southwest but they separate and pretend not to know one another. Eden, predictably, meets a young woman named Paula Wendell, and that establishes the formula light romance. Eden learns that Madden is supposedly at his ranch but no one has actually seen him. He travels there and recognizes Madden to whom he speaks, but Chan – posing as a servant in the house – silently warns him to play his cards close to his chest, so he claims that the pearls are to be sent only when he wires home to say that everything is all right. The parrot of the title is resident at the ranch. The parrot repeats words suggesting he was present for a murder but Madden makes little of it.

Paula Wendell is scouting for movie locations and appears with a letter from Madden authorizing her company to film on the property, but the secretary tells her that permission has been rescinded. She is obviously the romantic interest for Bob Eden despite being engaged to someone else. She wheedles Madden into renewing the permit but while she is there the talkative parrot is found dead. She also mention that she saw a bearded prospector at the ranch a few nights earlier. Both Eden and Chan independently discover that a revolver is missing from Madden's collection, and Chan finds a recent bullet hole in the wall of one room. Complicating matters further, Eden spots Maydorf during a brief visit to the nearby town.

Although Eden has seen Madden before and believes that is the person with whom he is dealing, there are multiple suggestions that he is an imposter. He agrees to an interview with a local newspaperman, which is completely out of character, and invites the photographer to stay for lunch, despite the clear objection of his secretary, who seems more like a manager than an assistant. The parrot's outburst suggests that the real Madden may have been killed before Chan and Eden arrived. Chan clandestinely searches the secretary's room and finds the missing revolver, with two empty chambers.

Louie Wong returns from San Francisco and is promptly stabbed to death before he can reach the ranch. The secretary and an unnamed man claiming to be a naturalist calling himself Gamble were in the vicinity at the time. Gamble later takes up temporary residency at the ranch. This will confirm to most readers that the Madden at the ranch is not the original despite looking amazingly like him. There is a slight misstep here, however. The local doctor, who rented a cottage to Maydorf under a false name, tells Madden that her tenant has disappeared and that he should tell the police. There is no logical reason why she, a local resident, would make a special trip to the ranch to ask someone else to talk to the local police.

Eden subsequently finds an old prospector who was at the ranch the day before he and Chan arrived and that he saw a man being shot, but he insists the assailant was Madden himself. This reinforces the theory that the Madden they met later is an imposter. The daughter, who was coming to visit, is met at the train station by the secretary and she disappears mysteriously. Then another visitor shows up who sees through the sham, and leaves town hastily moments later. The climax ends with the arrest of all four villains and the only surprise is that Madden is wounded but still alive.

Although quite entertaining, the novel has some serious structural problems. The rough outline of what is happening is too obvious too soon, and crucial evidence is discovered by happenstance. The chance of an actor who just happens to know Madden and his double appearing by happenstance at the crucial moment is just too convenient. The romantic interlude is overly long and disrupts the main plot at times. The stalling techniques by Eden and Chan are painfully obvious and must have raised an alarm with the villains. The alternate explanation for the events we have seen – the suggestion that Madden killed a blackmailer and concealed the body – loses all dramatic plausibility when it is espoused by Eden and a local newspaperman named Holley rather than by Chan, which shreds the last of its dubious credibility. Most of all, the story just goes on for too long.

Behind That Curtain (1928) was filmed in 1929 and remade in 1932 as *Charlie Chan's Chance*. A reporter named Rankin wants to bring together Charlie Chan and Sir Frederic Bruce, who recently retired from Scotland Yard and who is in San Francisco dealing with matters related to his memoirs. Sir Frederic is the guest of entrepreneur Barry Kirk, who has arranged a luncheon with June Morrow from the local district attorney's office and who suggests that Rankin and Chan join them.

Over lunch, Sir Frederic mentions that he has made a kind of hobby of the disappearance of Eve Durand, who went missing during an outdoor party in India. He believes he has figured out what happened, that Durand ran away and was not abducted, and he is close to finding her, but he is appalled when he realizes that their conversation on the subject might find its way into a newspaper story.

The same guests save only Rankin are invited to dinner, where they meet Kirk's grandmother and her companion, the Enderbys, a famous explorer named Beetham, and a retired actress named Garland. Not surprisingly, Sir Frederic is fatally shot, in this case while investigating a possible intruder. Mrs. Enderby in fact reports seeing someone leap from the fire escape and run off. Sir Frederic had been wearing a pair of slippers that were evidence in another famous case and they are missing. He seems to have been setting a trap since he removed all important papers from the office he was using, and then pointedly mentioned that he had left the safe unlocked during the early moments of the party. It was possible for people to come and go clandestinely because the lights were off so that Beetham could show movies of his exploration, but it is potentially significant that he suspended his commentary during one entire reel.

During the preceding conversations, we were introduced to the idea of the essential clue. This is supposedly based on a Scotland Yard belief - which Biggers probably invented – that one should figure out what the single most important clue is in a case and then virtually ignore the others while following up on that one. The slippers that were stolen were believed to be the essential clue in an earlier murder, but Chan has already suggested that the killer knew of the Scotland Yard policy and therefore deliberately planted a meaningless one – the slippers. So is their disappearance an essential clue, or a red herring?

Some small clues emerge. Miss Enderby has a rust stain on her dress that may have come from the fire escape. One of Miss Garland's pearls is found near the murder site, a room she has supposedly never entered. And Sir Frederic grasped a book issued by the Cosmopolitan Club at the moment of his death, perhaps trying to indicate who his assailant was. The dead man had also expressed interest in interviewing an inhabitant of Chinatown named Li Gung, and a young woman named Lila Barr, who works in the same building as houses the Kirk penthouse, was seen tearfully running from Sir Frederic's temporary office. Kirk tells Chan that Sir Frederic had been making inquiries about her.

Chan initially refuses to get involved with the case and plans to head home to Hawaii, but two incidents change his plan. First, June Morrow accuses him of running away from a difficult problem. Second, he overhears Beetham sending his servant on an extended vacation, and the servant is named Li Gung. The romantic pattern is repeated, this time Barry Kirk and June Morrow, effectively removing them both from suspicion. Chan also discovers that someone has been intercepting and reading Sir Frederic's mail, and by examining the fingerprints he learn that it was Barry Kirk's butler, Paradise, who was responsible.

Lila Barr presents a credible explanation of her tears – she had just had a fight with her fiancé. Garland's explanation of the wayward pearl is believable and leads to another mystery. Sir Frederic was interested in more than one missing woman and Garland was a friend of an actress who disappeared in Nice eleven years earlier. It appears that at least two of the female characters may not be who they claim to be. And then Mrs. Enderby tells Chan that she too was asked by Sir Frederic about a female friend who disappeared mysteriously several years earlier. Unlike the others, she confesses that she did see the missing friend that night, and that she is employed as the elevator operator for Kirk's building.

Chan starts to unravel things just past the midway mark. The elevator girl who was once a friend of Mrs. Enderby is the same woman who disappeared in Nice and presumably also the one who vanished in India. The husband of Eve Durand, the earliest disappearance, arrives from England but before he can identify the elevator operator, she disappears despite being under police surveillance. He does, however, inform Chan that Beetham was present the day his wife vanished. Subsequent evidence seems to prove that Beetham smuggled her out of India and the local police detective is ready to force a confrontation, hoping someone will confess to the murder.

Biggers has more surprises for us, however. The missing elevator girl is found and although she is two of the missing women, the abandoned husband says she is not his wife. Chan then unravels the last threads of the case in one of the most concise and well organized summings up in detective fiction. Durand was responsible for the unsolved murder and his wife's discovery of that fact is why she ran away. She is Eve Durand after all and the pretense by herself and her husband was pretense.

This is a skillfully constructed mystery that progressively introduces new puzzles each linked to what has gone before. The pacing is much better than in the first two books and there is almost a sense of inevitability about the sequence of events. There is one small flaw. The letter to Sir Frederic that was intercepted was replaced by a blank sheet of paper. This would have drawn attention to the letter, so it would have been much more sensible to simply destroy it. There is also an amusing factual error of no importance to the plot. Beetham at one point mentions having found a coin dated 7 A.D. This dating system was not introduced until the Sixth Century. Chan makes some very misogynistic pronouncements, but it is unclear whether this was Biggers speaking or part of his attempt to portray Chan as a man raised in a very old fashioned and rigidly defined Asian tradition. There is a mild cheat - withheld information that only Chan knows – but it is not a fatal flaw.

The Black Camel (1929) was filmed in 1931. Shelah Fane is an actress who has just passed her peak. She has rented a house in Hawaii while shooting part of a movie there, and is accompanied by her secretary, Julie O'Neill. Jim Bradshaw is a publicity agent assigned to the project. Among the cast members are Diana Dixon and Huntley Van Horn. The director is Val Martino. Alan Jaynes is a wealthy man who was present during their trip to the islands and who has proposed to her. Fane has become almost obsessed with a fortune teller named Tarneverro. Bradshaw and O'Neill are quickly identified as the romantic couple for this book. Although we are provided with no details, Fane is worried about an incident in her past which is related to the still unsolved murder of actor Denny Mayo. Three other characters of note are Bob Fyfe, who was once married to Fane and is apparently now working in Hawaii, and Rita and Wilkie Ballou, their mutual friends.

Fane apparently tells Tarneverro something crucial about the death of Mayo and he approaches Charlie Chan and says he may have important information for the police but that he cannot divulge it just yet. He also advises Fane not to marry Jaynes, who threatens violence against the fortune teller. There is a dinner party to which all are invited and, naturally, Fane is found stabbed to death in a pavilion near the beach.

Tarneverro tells Chan that Fane admitted having witnessed Mayo's murder and told him that the killer was presently in Hawaii, but she doesn't reveal his name. The explanation why she didn't tell the police at the time – she wanted to avoid the publicity – appears to be nonsensical, which is an annoying flaw in the set up, although subsequent revelations justify it. This would also seem to eliminate Jaynes as a suspect in that crime, although that doesn't necessarily mean that he didn't kill Fane for other reasons. He and Tarneverro, plus the romantic couple - who were together at the time - all seem unlikely suspects for either crime, since Tarneverro fully intended to expose the first killer if he could.

A smashed wristwatch suggests that Fane was killed at eight o'clock, when Van Horn, Martino, Jaynes, and Tarneverro were all together, but it is possible that the watch was adjusted to provide this alibi. Fane left a letter behind but before Chan can read it he is attacked in the darkness and the letter is stolen. Even though his assailant could not have left the room – wherein all the suspects have been gathered – Chan does not order a search made, which fails to ring true. Instead he begins a general interrogation. Physical evidence is slim. The murder weapon is missing as is the ornate pin with which the dead woman had fastened flowers to her dress and an emerald ring. There are footprints in the sand suggesting someone with very worn shoes may have been present around the time of the murder. The Ballous were married at about the time of Mayo's death, which might just be coincidence.

Chan and Tarneverro decide that the broken watch was probably reset to misrepresent the time of death, which wipes out all the alibis. They also find the missing letter, which turns out to be innocuous. The footprints are matched to a drunken beachcomber who refuses to reveal his real name. Fyfe, the ex-husband, confesses to having briefly met with Fane shortly before he was killed. The beachcomber is about to reveal what he overheard at the pavilion when Fyfe blurts out a confession – but it is clearly false and Chan points out that Fyfe is actually the only one with a solid alibi, since he was on stage at the real time of death. Nor was he present when the letter was stolen from Chan. The missing ring turns up in O'Neill's possession, but she explains that she was supposed to try selling it to a local jeweler. There are some red herrings, one involving a pair of pickpocketing exercises that are not entirely plausible.

Biggers uses a different tactic this time. The reader is shown a sequence which is concealed from Chan. The beachcomber blackmails Fyfe, revealing that he lied to Chan about what he overheard and suggesting that what was actually said would cause major difficulties for Fyfe. New evidence reveals that Jaynes probably lied as well, that he was in the vicinity of the pavilion at the time of the murder, and that the beachcomber may actually have entered through a window. Additionally, O'Neill's story about the emerald ring is contradicted by the butler, who saw the ring on the dead woman's hand long after she had supposedly given it away. This is eventually explained and it is a not particularly convincing red herring.

Chan next has reason to suspect Tarneverro, who has concealed the fact that he understands Chinese and may have lied in other instances. Jaynes claims that the evidence linking him to the pavilion was planted by Tarneverrro, who still has what appears to be a solid alibi. It becomes clear that he is also the man who assaulted Chan and that he was responsible for other bits of obfuscation and sabotage, but he seems to have no motive and the two people to whom he was apparently talking at the time of the murder are above suspicion. Part of the explanation comes to light when it is discovered that his real name is Arthur Mayo, brother of the murdered actor.

The resolution is somewhat wobbly. Fane herself killed Denny Mayo and confessed it to Tarneverro, which seems extremely unlikely. Fyfe was clearly lying when he confessed in order to protect her reputation, even though they had been divorced for ten years, which is also rather hard to believe. The killer was Fane's maid, barely mentioned throughout the story, who was formerly married to Mayo. The coincidence of both brother and maid being closely connected to the person who killed their husband or brother without suspecting anything is a bit too drastic to be credible.

There are some other minor problems sprinkled through the plot. Tarneverro destroys all of the pictures of his brother because there was a strong resemblance between the two of them and he did not want to be recognized. But several of the other characters knew Denny Mayo personally and would certainly have noticed if this was the case. Biggers offers a completely inadequate explanation that is mostly doubletalk. Some of the characters act illogically – particularly O'Neill and Fyfe. Tarneverro's elaborate campaign is similarly unnecessary and is included simply to misdirect the reader's suspicions. Fane's letter to Tarneverro asking him to forget what she told him becomes much less plausible once we know she had actually admitted to murder. Chan gets a crucial clue – he recognizes a young woman of whom the beachcomber has painted a portrait – completely by chance. On balance this was a tolerable but significantly flawed installment in the series.

Charlie Chan Carries On (1930) opens with the fatal strangling of an American tourist in his hotel room in London. Inspector Duff, whom we met in *Behind That Curtain*, is in charge of the case. Hugh Drake was one of a party of seventeen participating in a world tour conducted by Dr. Lofton. He was an elderly man, nearly deaf. Although his body is found in his bed, there is evidence that he was placed there after death. The killer left a small bag of pebbles beside the body. Drake is clutching a piece of watch chain with a key attached, presumably belonging to his assailant. The master key to the hotel rooms had disappeared earlier in the day. Lofton had argued with the dead man during the evening and one of his personal possessions was allegedly used to strangle Drake

Biggers introduces most of the tour members in short order. Of particular interest is Ronald Keane, who has been pretending to have had a military career and who was noticed on the wrong floor the previous evening by the night watchman. The watchman also encountered another man in the darkness and this one assaulted him, but is unable to provide his identity, although he does believe that he tore the pocket of the man's jacket. Although Duff is certain that some of them are not telling all they know, there is nothing strong enough to justify acting. One of them, Minchin, is a prominent American mobster, but he seems unlikely to be involved. In an authorial aside – a device Biggers had not previously employed – we are told that Drake's deafness would prove to be the cause of his murder.

After the party has left England, Duff discovers that one of the hotel employees was paid to conceal the fact that Drake had switched rooms that night with Honywood, another member of the party. This clearly suggests that Honywood was the real target. Drake was murdered by mistake and moved back to his own room where it was later discovered. Honywood is himself murdered while the tour is in France, although it was arranged to look like a suicide. He had left a sealed envelope with Mrs. Luce, another tourist, but it is stolen from her room the same day he dies. Inspector Duff arrives just as the French police are conducting their own investigation.

The French believe, or pretend to believe, that it was a suicide. The note, which Mrs. Luce had read, appears innocuous, a simple request that someone notify his wife, who is elsewhere in Europe. All of the tour members report that their rooms have been searched. Duff arranges to meet with the new widow, who tells him on the telephone that she knows who killed her husband but that he is traveling under an assumed name, unknown to her. Duff arranges for her to meet the party and identify the killer, but she is fatally shot as she stands beside him in an elevator, and the killer throws a bag of pebbles into the car. She carried a letter from her husband in which he mentions that he and Drake had swapped rooms because of a noise that kept him awake, and which the deaf Drake would not hear.

This leaves Duff with nine male suspects if we include one who had previously left the party, but possibly did not go far. One is the young male half of a very understated light romance, which usually means that he is innocent. Two others seem unlikely - the mobster, who is very open about his past, and Lofton, the guide, whom Honywood would surely have recognized much sooner.

Scotland Yard sends an undercover detective to shadow the party, and he is murdered while they are in Japan. Duff is off to Honolulu to meet the group there, and renew his acquaintance with Charlie Chan. Someone shoots Duff in the back through the window of Chan's office, so Chan quickly boards the liner carrying the tour back to the mainland, determined to solve the crime. Duff, fortunately, recovers.

Aboard ship, Chan makes minor progress until one night when the whole company gets together for a dinner. They begin revealing things they never told the police before – the strap used to kill Drake did not belong to Lofton after all. Several people lied, and one of them turns out to be a private investigator working on a divorce case. Despite multiple conflicting clues, Chan identifies the murderer. The bags of stones were symbolic of some bootleg diamonds that the Honywoods stole from the killer many years earlier. There is one particularly clever clue, a single word mentioned by the murderer in an innocuous context, that makes it clear that he did it.

One of the strengths of the Charlie Chan novels is that while they share many of the same conventions and devices, these are arranged on an underlying structure that varies significantly from book to book. In this case, for example, Chan does not even appear in the first half of the novel, while in others he was on the scene in the opening chapter. While one story might be confined to a narrow range of locations, others like this one cover multiple countries. Biggers was willing to experiment with his writing rather than just rely on a proven formula, and that is one of the signs of a superior writer.

Keeper of the Keys (1932) was unfortunately Biggers' last book. Chan is on the mainland when he meets Luis Romano, an opera conductor, on a train. Both have been invited to the home of wealthy businessman Dudley Ward, although neither has met him before. Romano is married to a woman who had once been Mrs. Dudley Ward. Her name is Ellen Landini and she is an opera diva, now separated from Romano. The intervening husbands were John Ryder and Frederic Swan. All of these individuals are to visit at Ward's house along with Hugh Beaton, while Landini and her latest infatuation have been sighted in nearby Reno.

One of Landini's flirtations was with Michael Ireland, who eventually ran off with her maid. They are married and live in Reno and the wife, Cecile, has told Ward that Landini secretly gave birth to his son and gave the child away. Ward wants to find the boy, who would now be eighteen. Landini and Beaton are also invited and show up with his sister and a mutual acquaintance named Dinsdale. With everyone in place, Landini is shot dead, found alone in a room with the murder weapon lying beside her. Chan notices immediately that two boxes of cigarettes have had their tops swapped. The dead woman is clutching a scarf, but it is not her own.

    Several of the suspects were gathered together when they heard the shot, although this doesn't necessarily mean anything in a mystery novel. Beaton overheard Landini asking someone to get her scarf, which was green, but instead she had a pink one. Red/green color blindness is an obvious explanation. Beaton is initially identified as Landini's sole heir. She was writing a letter to Ryder shortly before her death but it was burned in the fireplace. The murder weapon belonged to the victim and the money she was carrying is now in the possession of Romano, who claims she gave it to him.

    Ireland – who has arrived by landing his airplane in a small field behind the house - then claims that Swan had been blackmailing Landini for years and that she was about to tell him she would pay him no more. Chan believes that Swan is lying when he says he has no knowledge of a child, and that Romano is lying when he implies that he does. There is also some evidence pointing to the elderly Chinese servant as the killer, although the fact that he is knocked unconscious during the night suggests otherwise. Despite this, Chan indicates that he believes the servant killed Landini. In fact, he uncharacteristically leaps to conclusions several times during the course of the novel.

    Heaton's sister and the local sheriff provide us with the romantic couple for this book, so they are both above suspicion despite the evidence pointing toward her – which Chan characterizes as very damaging although it is in fact quite circumstantial. This was the author trying to widen the cast of suspicious characters, but it doesn't work well in this case. Chan also discovers that Landini's will was never signed, which means that Romano inherits everything, although it is unlikely that he could have known this. Chan interviews Landini's secretary, who confirms the blackmail allegation, but she also tells him that the dead woman's son was accidentally killed while still a teenager.

Chan makes a point of mentioning that Landini's dog appeared to be terrified by the sound of the airplane on the night she died, but showed no fear or reluctance to board it on the following day. He also begins a series of experiments that he admits are designed to find out which of the suspects is color blind, eliminating Swan almost immediately. Reinforcing his innocence, Swan becomes victim number two shortly thereafter. Eventually Chan proves that Ward is color blind, that the fatal shot was masked by the sound of the airplane, and that the Chinese servant fired another to mislead everyone about the time of death, out of a sense of obligation to the family. There is almost no cheating – Chan reveals that he found the second bullet only during the revelation – but Chan himself seems like a slightly different person than he was in the other five books.

Mention should be made of Biggers' characterization of Chan and numerous other Asian characters. It was probably quite advanced for his time. Chinese history and culture is described as admirable and sophisticated – although Biggers does not seem to have felt similar admiration for Japan. Chan is, obviously, a highly intelligent man and the fact that he has sent his oldest daughter off to college suggests that he is not encumbered by tradition, though he honors it. There is evidence that Biggers exerted effort to understand Chinese customs and portray them accurately. That said, he occasionally drifts into stereotype that undercut his position otherwise.

Had Biggers lived to write several more adventures of Charlie Chan, his name would probably be as familiar as Agatha Christie and Rex Stout. Despite his short career, however, he created a character who has entered the public conscious through movies and books and it is unlikely that he will ever be forgotten.

ELIZABETH DALY

Elizabeth Daly (1878-1967) was an American writer who produced mostly light verse and prose until she was 62 when her first detective novel, *Unexpected Night*, was published in 1940. It introduced Henry Gamadge, who would appear in fifteen more novels before Daly's death. Gamadge works in the field of authentication of old documents and books, has a black man named Theodore who runs his house, an assistant named Harold Bantz, and a cat named Martin – who dies late in the series and is replaced. Gamadge has a friend named Schenck who starts as an insurance inspector and then becomes an FBI agent. There is also a lawyer named Macloud who appears in several of the books. Gamadge is in his early thirties at the beginning of the series and marries Clara, who was a suspect in *Murders in Volume 2*, during the gap between that and the following book. Daly also wrote one non-detective novel, *The Street Has Changed*, which appeared in 1941. She is considered one of the last of the writers from the golden age of the detective story.

Unexpected Night (1940) opens with Henry Gamadge visiting Colonel Harrison Barclay, his wife, and their son Frederic. They are also expecting their nephew Amberley, who was a weak heart and who is not expected to live long, who is coming with his guardian, Eleanor Cowden, his sister Alma, and Hugh Sanderson, who are driving up at Amberley's insistence because he wants to spend a while working with a theater group. Amberley is about to turn twenty-one, at which point he will inherit a substantial fortune left by another aunt. In the event that he dies before coming of age, the money goes to some distant relatives in France whom Mrs. Barclay met only once.

Amberley is also expected to create his own will once he has received his inheritance which includes healthy gifts to Sanderson, his tutor, and Arthur Atwood, another cousin, whom the Barclays dislike. Alma would inherit everything if Amberley died intestate. Gamadge stays long enough to be introduced to the travelers, then returns to his own hotel. They arrive a while later and after going to their rooms, Amberley comes downstairs and tells the night attendant that he dropped his valuable cigarette case. The attendant,

Sam, says that he will look for it – he finds it easily and places it in a drawer – but is convinced that the young man was planning to meet someone.

In the morning, Amberley's body is found at the foot of a nearby cliff. His wristwatch suggests that he died just after two in the morning. He was carrying his will in his pocket, although it does not appear to have been signed, and it is missing when his body is found. He had been trying to get in touch with his cousin Arthur, but the phones are not working. Sanderson suggests that this might have been a pretense, that he had already arranged a rendezvous at the edge of the cliff.

Alma announces that she intends to honor the bequests even if the will is not found, or signed, but she will be unable to do so until she comes of age herself in another two years. They confirm that Amberley sent a message to Atwood on the night of his death, but it appears that there was no plan for Atwood to meet him before the following day. Almost half of the story passes before we meet Atwood and his wife, and Atwood denies at that point that there was any plan to meet the dead man during the night.

One of the cast members, Adrienne Lake, also died that evening, although her body was not discovered until shortly before Gamadge and the police arrive. It is never really explained why the state police detective takes Gamadge along with him to each interview since he has no official standing or relevant expertise. Lake was suffering from a toothache and may have taken an overdose of painkiller, although this seems very unlikely. Her roommate, Susie Baker, did not hear anything unusual during the night and she and George Rogers, another member of the troupe, had met Amberley in the past.

Baker says that she saw Atwood's car return to the theater group's camp at about three in the morning. Atwood claims he was just moving it to a different parking spot. The younger Barclay slips an enigmatic note under Alma Cowden's hotel room door. Gamadge rather awkwardly convinces Alma and Mrs. Cowden to play golf with him and someone unknown tries to hit Alma with a driven ball. This sequence does not seem plausible; the chances of a fatal strike are high, as are the chances that the assailant might have been seen. People wandering around a golf course with just a single club are noticeable and the person involved presumably had been following them for some time waiting for the right opportunity. He or she would have needed to be standing in the open for the ploy to have had any chance at all, and that would have made discovery almost certain. Mrs. Cowden claims that Arthur Atwood was a trick golfer and could have made the shot.

Fred Barclay appears right afterward and he and Alma are obviously not comfortable in each other's presence. Before they leave the course they run into Mrs. Barclay and Hugh Sanderson, both of whom are golfing by themselves and who were therefore potentially the source of the wayward ball.

Two thirds of the way through, Gamadge knows who the killer is, but can't say anything because he lacks evidence. This is a generally forgivable flaw in many detective novels for obvious reasons, but it does raise the question of whether or not actually confiding in the police might have led to an earlier conclusion, and in some cases whether that might actually have saved lives. In this case Gamadge is convinced that the killer might strike again, so the omission is significant.

Gamadge has had his assistant do some research in New York City and discovers that the daughter of a prominent family eloped with an actor. She had a son who sometimes worked as a female impersonator. Alma tells Gamadge that she has decided not only that she had decided not to honor her brother's missing will but that she wants to give away the money immediately. He tells her that this is legally possible – it is not - but cautions her to think the matter over. It is in any case an invalid document and Gamadge only prepares it to calm her down.

Gamadge and the police attend the first performance of the play, during which Atwood is shot and killed. It is supposed to look like suicide but no one is fooled. Alma is poisoned with morphine, as was Adrienne Lake, but survives. Then Gamadge explains what really happened.

Amberley died before arriving at the hotel. Her aunt, Atwood, and Sanderson had developed a contingency plan in advance. Atwood drove down and impersonated the dead man at the hotel, after which Amberley's body was thrown from the cliff and Atwood drove back to the theater. The handwriting in Amberley's check book did not match his signature when he registered at the hotel.

Parts of the explanation are hard to accept. Atwood was taking the place of Adrienne Lake, whose toothache was so bad that she had been unable to rehearse. But Atwood paid her to impersonate herself during a lengthy rehearsal so that he could sneak off site. One could accept the fact that he could drive off undetected – although we have been previously told that his car is so noisy that this would have been impossible – but there is no possible way that people who knew them both could have been fooled in close proximity for several hours of rehearsal. The discrepancy in handwriting is a blatant example of withheld information, known to the detective but never revealed to the reader. It also turns out that a policeman saw Sanderson carrying a stolen porter's uniform with which he opened the door to Alma's room, another fact known only to Gamadge.

Atwood poisoned Lake who had provided him with the false alibi. Sanderson hit the golf ball in an attempt to frighten Alma, but it is not clear why he wished to do so, nor is it ever really explained why he drove up to the theater to kill Atwood. Sanderson's motive is not explained either since in none of the scenarios would he have gained more than a symbolic amount of money.

There are some other rough spots, not unusual in a first novel. There aren't enough conversational tags and during several of the three way discussions it is not always clear who is speaking. There are also some awkward jumps in which a sequence of events moves from first to last without any intermediary steps, which is both disorienting and distracting. This is sometimes done to avoid revealing too much to the reader too soon, but in some cases it serves no purpose at all.

Deadly Nightshade (1940) takes Gamadge from his New York office back to Maine at the request of the detective he helped in his first book. A group of children ate poison berries apparently given to them by a gypsy child and some of them have died. A local policeman died in an apparent accident the same day the children became ill. The detective, Mitchell, isn't very informative over the telephone but he stokes Gamadge's interest and he agrees to come.

One of the children who recovered was Tommy Ormiston, son of an artist who has eccentric ideas about employing domestic help and who has brought along some young people to maintain his home for room and board rather than wages. These include Miss Strangways, another artist who acted as cook, and Davidson Breck, who works in advertising and who looked after the children as well as doing much of the physical work. Tommy disappeared the morning they were preparing to go home, and a few of the belladonna berries were found where he was last seen. He was found unconscious in the woods a short time later. Tommy insists that he was given the berries by a strange lady in a car. His testimony is somewhat dubious because he is only six and because belladonna causes hallucinations.

The second child affected was Sarah Beasley, seven years old, who was at home with her older sister and a baby. Sarah went out to the barn to play with a new litter of cats and when her mother went looking for her, she was missing, as was one of the bells that she habitually hung around the necks of the kittens. Belladonna berries are found in the barn and nearby. She is still missing when Gamadge arrives.

Julia Bartram is the third victim. She lived at the family estate owned by her father, Carroll Bartram. His brother George and his family had recently arrived from Europe, having decided to relocate because of the unsettled state of affairs following the outbreak of the war. Julia disappeared from her house and was found lying unconscious in the woods. Because of a sensitivity to belladonna, which she was found holding, she died a few hours later. The three houses are so far apart that there is no chance that one child wandered among all three of them. A young boy living at the gypsy camp suffered the same symptoms, but the gypsies insist he just had a bout of influenza.

Except for Mitchell and Carroll Bartram, the locals all blame the gypsies, assuming the gypsy boy was the one who brought the belladonna to each location. Gamadge speculates that it was an adult who was responsible, that one of the children was targeted and the other two poisoned only as camouflage, chosen because of their accessibility at that particular time. He and Mitchell visit the gypsies and one of the children, William, admits that a lady in a car offered him a piece of candy, but stops talking when Gamadge tries to learn more.

His first real success is with the dead child's young cousin Irma. Left alone with her briefly, he entices her with talk about kittens and she reveals her prizes- a belladonna berry and the missing bell and ribbon from Sarah Beasley's house. She found both very close to where Julia was discovered lying comatose.

A meeting with the older Bartrams reveals little, although it includes the presentation to young Irma of the family jewels, formerly belonging to Julia, with the caution that they really aren't worth very much. Gamadge also learns that when the Bartram brothers' father died, there were almost half a million dollars missing from his estate. At one point he had purchased a large lot of paintings in Europe, but at a very low price, and they were later resold to Ormiston for the same amount.

The visit to the Ormistons provides some interesting information. Tommy, the boy who recovered, is not their child at all. Strangways – whose real name is Walworth - is his mother, but the family keeps up the pretense that Tommy is one of their own. Ormiston has a very low opinion of the gypsies and insists that they were responsible – perhaps inadvertently – for the poisonings. Strangways' husband recent died in prison after poisoning an entire family. The survivor of that poisoning, Evelyn Walworth, has only recently been released from an asylum. Strangways tells Gamadge that Emily is staying in the area and has asked to see her. Years earlier, Emily had accused her of being the poisoner rather than her husband. She meets with Strangways in Gamadge's presence and indicates that she now recognizes that she was delusional.

Mrs. Beasley mentions that there was a woman taking photographs of children for some sort of magazine competition, but Gamadge suspects this is a ruse and suggests that the woman was actually Evelyn Walworth in disguise. It turns out that she had visited all three families with the same story. Gamadge spends a lot of time talking to Dr. Loring, who is very close to the Bartram family.

Once again Gamadge claims to know who is responsible two thirds of the way through the story, and once again he refuses to confide his theory to the police because he has insufficient evidence. This is the point at which Daly believes that a reader ought to be able to figure out the solution, but in fact it would be complete guesswork. We have not yet been provided with essential clues.

An insurance investigator shows up, concerned because the Ormistons have taken out insurance policies on both Tommy and his mother, Strangways. I believe that by 1940 it was already necessary to have an insurable interest in someone, so the second of these policies would probably never have been issued, a point apparently unknown to the author.

Gamadge uses code words to communicate with his assistant and directs him to seek information back in New York City. This device recurs in the next book and then disappears. Then someone pretending to be Mrs. Ormiston calls and says Strangways is missing and when Gamadge and Mitchell drive to the scene, they are almost ambushed by someone who distracted them by placing a dummy in the road. Gamadge concludes that this is the ploy that caused the fatal accident to the policeman on the day of the poisonings.

A search of Evelyn Walworth's car produces a revolver and a camera. Strangways and Breck take Tommy and set off for New York after an argument with Ormiston. Harold, the assistant, provides various cryptic messages that Gamadge doesn't immediately explain, which is an obvious case of withheld information, very unfair to the reader. The resolution ties up the questions about the missing money, and there is a very nice twist in which we discover that Bartram never had a daughter, that he had intended to borrow a drugged Sarah Beasley for that purpose. Unfortunately Dr. Loring, who was part of the conspiracy, miscalculated the dosage and killed her.

This was a much better novel that Daly's first effort. There are a trifle too many characters and it is occasionally difficult to keep the various servants, children, and other relatives separate. The problem with conversational tags was no longer serious and Gamadge was beginning to assume a definite personality. The explanation, however, is marred somewhat by missing details about how the various parts of the plan were carried out.

Murders in Volume 2 (1941) opens with the arrival of Robina Vauregard who wants Gamadge to look into a matter involving the fourth dimension. Her uncle Imrie – who is quite elderly – apparently believes in it and the family is concerned that he is being manipulated by confidence men. Her sister is Angela Morton, an actress who is married to Tom Duncannon. Dick Vauregard and Clara Dawson, nephew and niece respectively, are both in their twenties, orphaned, and live with the rest of the family. Clara is romantically involved with Cameron Payne. Imrie and Angela are the only ones with money and they support the younger members of the family in a house separate from Imrie's.

One hundred years earlier, a female tutor went out into the walled garden at the Vauregard residence with volume two of the works of Byron, and was never seen again. No member of the family has entered the garden since that day. Now Imbrie has a houseguest whom, he says, walked out of the garden carrying the missing book, dressed anachronistically and claiming to be the woman who disappeared a century earlier. She is clearly a well rehearsed imposter but the elderly Vauregard is taken in and the family is afraid to upset him by challenging her authenticity.

There are clues early on suggesting the woman, Miss Smith, is part of a conspiracy. She refers to things that did not exist a century earlier, and upon arriving she promptly burns the clothes that she was wearing, even raking out the coals and disposing of them. Vauregard is keeping her story secret, having told the household staff that she is a refugee from the war in Europe. Gamadge, however, tells Robina that he is convinced that Miss Smith is working with a member of the family, probably in an attempt to divert the elderly man from a plan to distribute a portion of his fortune outside the family. Robina accepts that the motive might be well intentioned but feels that it is still fraudulent and ill conceived.

Angela had briefly been caught up in an occult group called New Soul and introduced Imrie to it before she lost interest. Imrie remained in touch although he has not attended any meetings since Miss Smith materialized. New Soul is run by Mr. & Mrs. Chandor. Gamadge also meets Bridge, who is directing a new play which will star Angela. On a pretext, he visits the Dykincks, elderly mother and unmarried daughter, who were once friends of the Vauregards and who have a set of Byron identical to the one at the Vauregard house. Their set is missing the second volume, which presumably is the one Miss Smith was carrying. It doesn't take long for Gamadge to figure out that the daughter is a party to the conspiracy.

Gamadge believes that he has uncovered enough evidence to convince Imrie that he is being fooled, but when he arrives to speak to him he finds the man dead in his library. He has been poisoned and the missing book, which had been returned, is missing again. So is Miss Smith. Gamadge then receives a call from Angela Morton asking him to come to her house to discuss the case, and he arrives to find that she has been strangled during the interim. Shortly afterward he determines that the poison was probably stolen from the family's veterinarian.

Gamadge seems to have figured things out but he is not

volunteering any information until he can prove his charges. It has been apparent for some time that Miss Dykinck provided the mysterious book to a gentleman caller, who is someone we know, and that Angela Morton was part of a conspiracy to fool Imrie into thinking Miss Smith was genuine in order to divert him from plans to make a major bequest to the New Soul cult. He is also convinced that Cameron saw the killer leave Imrie's garden and tries to warn the man that his life is in danger.

There is a good deal of running about toward the end. Gamadge is trying to protect Cameron, who has been blackmailing the killer, who turns out to be Dick Vauregard, who is secretly married to the actress who posed as Miss Smith. Dick dies accidentally while trying to sneak back into his house to avoid police scrutiny and his wife is apprehended shortly thereafter.

The premise is quite clever, even though we know from the outset that fraud is involved. Daly has improved her story control and the succession of scenes flows logically from one to the next. Unfortunately it begins to falter toward the end, in part because there are too few characters this time for there to be much of a mystery and partly because Daly apparently could not think of an ending as clever as her opening. It is still, however, a reasonably good detective story.

The House Without the Door (1942) opens with Gamadge's visit to Vina Gregson, who was acquitted of murdering her husband and now lives in seclusion, her only friend being Minnie Stoner who lives nearby. The two of them spend half of each year in the city and the other half at Gregson's secluded country house, where they live together. She has been receiving vaguely threatening letters which imply that she might be guilty of murder despite the jury's decision in her favor.

The only visitors they entertain are Cecilia Warren, Gregson's cousin, and Benton Locke, her late husband's adopted son. Gregson has been living under an assumed name and the letters have come via her banker from her old address. They were all visiting the house the night that Gregson's husband died. Cecilia has been seeing Paul Belden and Locke has an informal relationship with Arline Prady. There has also been a series of accidents of suspicious nature. Grease was spread at the top of a dangerous flight of stairs, there was a dubious case of food poisoning, and someone turned on the gas with the pilot light off and sent a poisoned cake. The last two were clearly not accidents.

Gamadge – who is now married to Clara from the previous book - is inclined to dismiss the four attempts as fakes because Gregson survived them all, but at least three of them could have been fatal so this conclusion seems unwarranted. The bulk of her estate if she died would be split between Warren and Locke. Gamadge assumes that Gregson believes that the person who killed her husband is behind the attacks and recommends that she temporarily change her will and move to a private rest home while he investigates.

Gamadge then relates the story of Curtis Gregson's death. He died of an overdose of morphine which many believed he took himself, although there is no discernible reason why he would have wanted to commit suicide. The evidence against his wife was chiefly that another member of the household heard the victim laugh in the middle of the night.

Gamadge convinces Gregson to go into hiding. He plans to visit the house where Stoner is staying and finds Locke's body nearby, shot to death. He interprets this as another attempt to blacken Gregson's reputation although she could not possibly have been responsible. He moves the body to divert suspicion. The next day Mrs. Smiles, an elderly woman who employs Cecilia as a companion, invites all of the interested parties to dinner at her house.

Gamadge's wife Clara finds the handgun that killed Locke concealed in the closet in Cecilia's room. Gamadge reveals this discovery to the assembled party, then cryptically tells them that he is concealing it so the police won't find it, and that he knows they will come with a search warrant because an earlier conversation with a police detective mentioned that they had received an anonymous note related to the case. Clearly the gun was planted to implicate Cecilia in the murder of Locke.

This is one of those mysteries where the villain is above suspicion, i.e., it is the supposedly menaced Mrs. Gregson, who did in fact poison her husband. Despite her acquittal, her name is still tainted and she wants to frame one of her heirs for the crime. Gamadge insists that he saw through this right from the start, although that didn't do Locke any good. Part of the solution is rather unconvincing. We were told how secure the rest home where she is hiding is, that she would be watched over by staff and secretly by

Gamadge's assistant as well, but she still manages to sneak off at least twice unobserved, and there seems to be no plausible way she could have planted the murder weapon in Mrs. Smiles' apartment. There is also a good deal of withheld information. This was not one of Daly's successful novels.

Nothing Can Rescue Me (1946) opens with Henry Gamadge accepting an invitation to spend a weekend with Sylvanus Hutter and his aunt Florence while his own wife is visiting a sick aunt. Florence is married to the much younger Tim Mason. Her secretary is Evelyn Wing. Other houseguests include Sally Deedes, who has interested Florence in the occult, Susie Bert, and Glen Percy, both friends of the family. Corinne Hutter, a cousin, arrives the same day as Gamadge so presumably could not be responsible for the earlier incidents. Florence has been working on a novel recently and that is the focus of the strange events they want investigated. Florence and Sylvanus are supported by a trust fund and if Florence should die, he would inherit the entire fortune.

The mystery is that someone is adding famous quotes to the novel manuscript surreptitiously, and the quotes can be interpreted as threatening. Gamadge stirs things up a bit and hears rumors that Mason has been flirting with Burt, that Wing has been spying on the family and reporting to Florence, and that Sylvanus may be an alcoholic.

Sylvanus is murdered, bludgeoned to death, which means that Florence is now worth millions of dollars. At Gamadge's urging, she writes a new will with the bulk of her money going to charity to prevent it all going to Wing. Evidence is uncovered that the killer used Percy's overcoat and hat while committing the crime and burned something in the garden. Only Florence has a viable alibi, since she was with Gamadge at the time. The only person with no motive is Corinne Hutter, which is in itself suspicious.

Not surprisingly, Florence is poisoned later that same day despite the presence of a nurse in her room. Her medication was readily available and everyone had the opportunity to adulterate it. Although it is not clear how the guilty party – Corinne Hutter – hoped to gain anything until after her guilt is revealed, the fact that she is the least likely to have committed the crime – apparently lacking both motive and opportunity – points strongly to her guilt. There would otherwise be no purpose to her presence in the story.

Although this was overall a good mystery, it has some minor problems. The accounts of where people were at the time Sylvanus was murdered are so muddled and incomplete that it is difficult to analyze them. There are also lapses of Daly's early habit of not providing adequate conversational tags, requiring the reader to skip back and count exchanges to discover who is saying what.

Evidence of Things Seen (1943) focuses on Gamadge's wife Clara initially. She is staying in a summer cottage where she expects her husband and another couple, the Herons, to join her shortly. She and her housekeeper have been puzzled by the appearance of a mysterious female figure who periodically is seen apparently watching the cottage from a distance. They buy fresh eggs from the owner of the cottage, Miss Alvira Radford, who recently inherited a substantial sum of money from her sister. Clara has noticed two odd things about the cottage. There is a door to one room that seems to have opened itself, and another door to the outside that has been painted over and is locked tight. Radford's sister, who bequeathed her the money, died in the cottage.

Clara meets Hattie Groby, who is Alvira's niece, and her husband Walt, who runs a garage and is rumored to be a petty criminal. She inquires about the identity of the woman whom she has seen from a distance but no one can imagine who it might be. The fact that she is wearing clothes very similar to those of the dead sister, whose possession are in the attic of the cottage, suggests a connection. Not too far distant are Phineas and Fanny Hunter, who are friends of the Gamadges. They tell Clara that there were rumors that Alvira poisoned her sister for her money. Another friend in the area is Gilbert Craye, who is something of a social outcast because of his contrariness.

There is the aura of the supernatural when Alvira shows up at the cottage, which she refuses to enter, with her horse and buggy. The mysterious woman appears and the horse panics, wrecking the buggy and knocking Alvira unconscious. That night, Clara sees the strange woman in the house and Alvira is found to have been fatally strangled. The Hunters are also staying at the cottage and they help her deal with the police, who are convinced that Clara is imagining things.

This is the point at which Gamadge arrives. Clara tells him that she saw the strange figure clearly, but that the intruder never went into the room where Alvira was killed. Everyone assumes that Clara hallucinated or dreamed parts of her story but Gamadge believes her and is determined to find out the truth.

Hattie Groby inherits Alvira's entire estate, but neither she nor her husband seem to be bright enough to have engineered the murder. Gamadge investigates in a slow moving sequence of chapters, and some of his information is gained almost by accident. Several of the characters are kept at a distance so that it is hard to draw any impression of them. Gamadge's repeated insistence that Clara might be judged legally insane because her account of the crime does not make sense is ridiculous. This was far inferior to her previous novels, both in construction and in pacing.

Arrow Pointing Nowhere (1944) has another intriguing opening. Someone has been leaving cryptic notes outside the Fenway house, at least one of them clearly meant for Henry Gamadge. The mailman finds them and reports up through channels and eventually Gamadge is advised of the situation. The notes appear to have been written by someone with no access to ordinary writing paper, presumably a prisoner – a device which Daly will use more than once in the future. Gamadge knows of the Fenways slightly but has not met them. Blake Fenway is the head of the family, Living with him are his unmarried daughter Caroline, his brother's widow Belle and her adult son Alden, and an elderly cousin, Mott Fenway. Alden has never progressed beyond the age of six mentally. Belle is temporarily using a wheelchair because of an accident. Alice Grove is Belle's companion and aide and lives with them. A newspaper reporter recovering from a serious illness and the companion's niece Hilda are also resident.

The family is supported largely by the income on a trust fund. Half of that fund was settled on Alden before his mental deficiency was evident. The other half pays its income to Blake and the capital will go to Caroline upon his death. Gamadge's preliminary investigation indicates that Blake, his daughter, Alden, and the reporter, Bill Craddock, are all free to come and go as they please so presumably none of them are the author of the notes.

Gamadge uses a mutual interest in collectible books to arrange a visit to the household. Hilda, according to Blake, is at the family's second home overseeing the shipment of valuable books to the main house. This would seem to rule her out as the prisoner, unless Blake is lying. Blake also tells him that they have a small mystery; an inset plate in a rare book which showed the old family house, long since torn down, has been torn out and has disappeared. It is not clear if this happened over the course of twenty years or within the past few days.

When Gamadge takes his leave, Mott surreptitiously requests a short, private conversation. He explains that there is tension between Belle and Caroline, who are both strong minded, and that the tension may lie behind a series of small incidents. Caroline's dog is found with its skull crushed, but it might have gotten outside and been hit by a passing automobile. Mott says that he believes that Alden is deteriorating and probably stole the page from the book and talks Gamadge into coming back after dark to search for it. This is not a particularly plausible scenario.

Gamadge confers with his assistant. Their working theory is that the messages were sent by Belle, probably because she is being blackmailed about something Alden did. Gamadge visits the country home and for some reason concludes that Craddock may have brought the missing photograph and hidden it there. Upon returning to the city, he arranges to meet with Mott but Mott "falls" to his death from an open window beforehand. Caroline then tells him that she thinks Alden killed the dog, stole the photo, and murdered Mott.

Craddock tells Gamadge that Mrs. Grove is the villain and another anonymous note – whose delivery relies on extraordinary luck – convinces Gamadge to lure Alice away from the country home long enough for it to be searched. The search turns up a death trap and Gamadge's assistant, Harold, believes that Craddock set it up. By this point the reader may be understandably confused, but in part this is because no one including Gamadge seems to be acting rationally. We also learn that some of the prints in the damaged book bear imprints of letters written on top of them – it is not clear why anyone would have done this – and the implication is that the missing plate bore similar marks. Nor is there any explanation for why Caroline believes that the existence of the marks is in itself terribly upsetting regardless of their import.

There is an argument between Mrs. Groves and Belle. Belle is shot and wounded but Mrs. Groves is killed, apparently by Alden who came to the aid of his mother. Belle insists that Groves was trying to extort money from her and had told her that there was a deathtrap at the other house. It is never explained why this would put pressure on Belle to pay. Belle also insists that she did not have much money, but that also makes no sense because Alden was in possession of half the trust fund. And Gamadge implies that Alden will be institutionalized now, but he seems to have acted in the defense of his mother, who was being threatened with death. In fact he is not mentally ill at all. He is an imposter and he and his "mother" have been conducting a fraud.

Although this was an improvement over the previous book, it has continuity problems and a terrible conclusion. The impressions in the picture indicate that the original Alden died and the present one is adopted, and not mentally impaired. The chances that someone could pull this off over the course of years in close quarters with several other people defies belief. There is no evidence presented to support this in advance which makes the resolution an extended and major cheat. Gamadge and some of the other characters embark on courses of action that seem random, and draw conclusions based on no apparent evidence at all. Grove sent the anonymous notes, but there was no reason for her to do so. Despite an attempt to justify this by explaining that she could not have left without causing a scene, this is an absurd explanation of her confinement and secrecy.

Reclusive Mr. Crenshaw, fatally ill, is dying in the hospital in the opening chapters of *The Book of the Dead* (1944). Crenshaw's only companion is Pike, an unemployed man whom he met while in New Hampshire and who has been serving as his valet/nurse. Idelia Fisher met Crenshaw during his trip north and liked him but she got the impression that he was afraid of Pike. He left a book of plays by Shakespeare with her and certain marked passages and some rubbed out writing puzzle her so she goes to see Gamadge. They decide to visit the hospital, only to learn that Crenshaw has died of leukemia that very day.

Gamadge talks to Crenshaw's doctor, Billig, and learns nothing new, but as soon as he leaves the doctor rushes out even though it is late at night. There is clearly some sort of conspiracy involving Billig and Pike. A short time later Gamadge finds Fisher dead, her skull crushed. He reports it anonymously and goes home, only to find an intruder waiting for him. Narrowly escaping death, Gamadge still refrains from voicing any suspicions of a connection to the police.

A woman shows up claiming to be Crenshaw's widow, which is strange since he had claimed to have neither friends nor relatives to notify. She is accompanied by her niece, Lucette Daker. Mrs. Crenshaw announces her immediate departure for home in California, but Daker insists that she is staying in New York and confides to Gamadge that she has a secret boyfriend whom she is meeting and that they are going to get married. Meanwhile, Mrs. Crenshaw mysteriously does not board the train that she is supposed to be taking. This is a red herring as we later learn that she stayed in New York at Gamadge's request, a clear case of withheld information.

Schenck meanwhile has been checking up on Pike and the story about how he met Crenshaw is obviously false. Gamadge hires private detectives to follow Billig, who makes clandestine visits to the street outside Gamadge's home, and openly visits a private nursing home. Then Pike takes off and is tracked to a remote inn where he goes by the name Maxwell. Mrs. Maxwell turns out to be Daker. But since Crenshaw undoubtedly did die of leukemia and not murder, what is the nature of the conspiracy?

The surprise revelation is that Maxwell/Pike is actually the real Crenshaw. The dead man was his cousin who looked a lot like him. Crenshaw wanted a divorce so that he could run off with Daker but his wife would not consider it. Initially it looks as though the only crime he can be convicted of is perpetrating fraud through the mail – which is dubious at best – but then one of Fisher's possessions turns up which ties him to her murder. Daker agrees to testify against him. This was a quite pleasant novel with an interesting puzzle and some surprising twists and turns. It was her best work to date.

Any Shape of Form (1945) introduces Gamadge's elderly cousin Abby, whose friends include Walt and Blanche Drummond. They have all been invited to a party held by John Redfield, who has recently installed a rather ugly object d'art in his garden. Redfield's own Aunt Josephine is the guest of honor. Also invited are David and Cora Malcolm, her stepchildren, who were estranged when she married their father, now deceased. They have never previously met. Archibald Malcolm left a substantial estate, but the children will see little of it until after Josephine dies.

Josephine has become fascinated with what we would now call New Age cults, astrology, predestination, etc. Gamadge is talking to her in the garden when she is fatally shot from ambush. The murder weapon is a rifle which some members of the party had been using to shoot crows a short time before. The brother and sister are in line for a very large inheritance and Redfield expects a substantial one as well. He also reveals that the dead woman recently fired her long time companion under tense circumstances.

The interviews hint at a romantic relationship between Walt Drummond and Cora, and between his wife and her brother. Cora freely admits that they disliked their stepmother and that they are now going to be rich because of her death. Only Abby appears to have a good alibi – she was too far away at the time the shot was fired – and the others all had plenty of opportunity. The fact that David Malcolm married the woman who nursed him through a serious head injury has been mentioned, as well as the fact that they are separated, but she is absent until she unexpectedly shows up shortly after the murder is committed, apparently intent upon making sure she benefits from any financial windfall.

That evening the wife, Frederica, is bludgeoned to death in a guest bedroom. This eliminates her as a suspect, obviously, and since the Malcolms are too clearly suspects for the wary reader to believe them responsible, there are only three real possibilities. Walt Drummond is very fond of Cora and Blanche is infatuated with David, who admits that they had a short lived affair. Blanche has been unhappy in her marriage for several years. Daly clearly expects us to suspect Blanche – who found the body, convinced Frederica to stay at the house rather than the hotel, and who is aware that Donald has never been divorced.

Cora lost a distinctive piece of jewelry at about the time of the first murder, but it is never mentioned again until Gamadge assembles the company and finds it at the murder scene. This was obviously planted and by now the experienced reader will have likely decided correctly that Redfield committed both murders. He is known to have a small inheritance coming, but more importantly he has embezzled a good deal of Josephine's money – which is a mild cheat since the reader had no way of knowing about that crime. Although this is no surprise when all is revealed, Daly has some other twists – most directly the fact that the Josephine who was shot was an imposter, was actually her long time companion who supposedly was discharged for no clear reason. Gamadge determined this in part by examining the clothing in her room, some of which doesn't fit, a fact which is never conveyed to the reader. She was blackmailing Redfield because she knew of the embezzlement and hoped to acquire more – by some dubious and never clearly described plan – before revealing that Josephine is dead.

Clara's absence this time is explained by the birth of their son. There is some very mild racial stereotyping in the section dealing with the hired help. The solution is a mixture of the obvious and the surprising, but the latter depend too much on withheld information. Despite that problem, this was a competent mystery and marked the beginning of the best period in Daly's career. The missing piece of jewelry also has some minor significance which the reader would not guess without familiarity with something called a Regard Pin, and even then might be confused because the sequence of stones is incorrectly stated when it is being described.

Somewhere in the House (1946) is one of Daly's best novels. Gamadge is hired by Harriet Leeder to be present when her family opens a room that has been sealed for twenty years. Her grandmother had been obsessed with one daughter, Nonie, who died in her thirties, and an effigy of the dead woman was installed at a piano in the room. The terms of the grandmother's will include instructions that nothing in the house be changed and that all of her heirs live there during a twenty year period. Leeder states her concern that a valuable collection of buttons may have been concealed in the room and does not want one of the other family members to steal them.

Those other family members include her Uncle Gavan and Aunt Cynthia, another uncle named Seward and his college aged daughter Elena, and an orphan cousin named Garth. An informal member of the household is Harriet's ex-husband Rowe Leeder, whom she was pressured into divorcing after he became a suspect in the murder of a woman named Sillerman at about the time of Nonie's death. He had an alibi and is still named in the will and is on good terms with the family. Garth and Elena were both young children at the time of Nonie's death, about which there is no suspicion of wrongdoing. Elena is romantically involved with Donald Malcolm from *Any Shape or Form*, who has now become Gamadge's assistant, and the couple are married at the end of the novel.

We also are told the history of Aggie Fitch, a distant relative who was companion to the grandmother but detested by the rest of the family. Fitch disappeared right after the grandmother's funeral and neither she nor her other relatives – the Nagles – ever heard from her again. She had drawn out all of her savings and had been talking about a world cruise, so no one became concerned until it was too late. Only the most inexperienced reader will fail to guess that her body is concealed inside the hermetically sealed room.

By mutual agreement, Gamadge is the only one to enter the room when it is unsealed, and he finds the body immediately. Leeder has also mentioned by now that several valuable artifacts have disappeared from the house over the course of years, and that the family never contacted the police because they feared this would invalidate the terms of the will. Again, Elana and Garth are too young to have been responsible, at least for the earliest of the thefts.

Several people in the house make a hobby of converting old books into boxes, called solanders. This is emphasized so strongly that it is obvious that there is some significance to them. Part of this is quite sensible – one of the murder weapons, a revolver, is concealed in one and when it is eventually discovered – after Garth becomes the latest victim – the ballistics match those of the bullet that killed the Sillerman woman. She was notorious for procuring drugs and other illicit objects for anyone who had the money. Garth brought doom on himself by following someone from the house to a secret apartment in the city. The weapon that killed Fitch, a lamp wire, is also concealed in a solander. There is a weak attempt to suggest that the Nagles are viable suspects, but it is never plausible.

Gamadge notices that one of the converted books is an account of adventures in India that included a description of thuggee assassination methods, and it matches the way Fitch was killed. This is a bit of a reach since strangulation with a cord is hardly specific to India. More through intuition than evidence, Gamadge concludes that Harriet Reeder is the killer, that Rowe has been protecting her for many years, and he sets up a trap to cause her to implicate herself. She promptly commits suicide. One of the devices of the detective story is to make the client the actual killer – most notably in John Dickson Carr's *Below Suspicion* – and it works effectively here.

The Wrong Way Down (1946) was something of a departure because this time the reader is presented with a situation in which all of the characters seem to be part of the murderous conspiracy, and it is just a question of which of them committed which act. Daly has a surprise in store for us, however. Things are not what they appear to be.

Julia Paxton is an elderly relative of James Ashbury, who lives on the west coast but has inherited an old family house in New York. Paxton, who shares almost equally with Ashbury in the disposal of a fairly substantial estate, offers to live in the house temporarily and to dispose of the contents in as profitable a manner as possible. Paxton is aided only by Mrs. Keate, a cleaning lady who is only there for a few hours each week. Paxton is a friend of Gamadge's wife Clara, who has gone to Florida for the winter, and he stops by to make a courtesy visit.

Paxton presents Gamadge with a problem. Shortly after a visit from a cousin, Iris Vance, one of the engravings in the house is subtly altered. Vance was a medium as a child, although it turns out she had long since disavowed any supernatural powers. Gamadge concludes that she has stolen the original and substituted a copy, and decides to confront her. In her apartment, he is introduced to two men and two women besides Vance, some or all of them obviously using fake names, and he concludes that two of them are in fact the grown children of James Ashbury. Vance denies having stolen the engraving, but there are obvious tensions, and as Gamadge is leaving, someone tries to shoot him in the back, saved only because Harold Bantz – returned to Gamadge's service following the war – fires at the assailant.

It appears like that the assassin was one of the foursome, the man going under the name Bowles. Paxton has already been killed in what appears to be an accidental fall. Gamadge goes to the police, but although Iris Vance and the young couple are cooperative, Bowles and the other woman, Spiker, are nowhere to be found. The police call Ashbury Senior, who reluctantly admits that his children are in Ne w York City, although he is apparently surprised to discover that they know Vance.

The obvious motive in Paxton's death is her share of the inheritance, but why would Ashbury have involved his children and three other people in the plot? He agrees to come to New York and the police begin an exhaustive search for Bowles. There is considerable running around before Spiker turns up, shot to death on Gamadge's doorstep. He is now convinced that the substitution of the picture had nothing to do with the murder, that it was unrelated except that it brought him into the case. This proves to be true. It is less clear why the attempts are being made on his life, since he has already told the police everything he knows. But there is an excellent reason.

There is a quite clever ending which readers are unlikely to anticipate. We have been told that Ashbury's second wife is bedridden. What we don't know is that she is a drug addict and a psychopath, that she murdered Paxton and Spiker, and tried to kill Gamadge. The reason he has to die is that he is the only living person who has seen her in her disguise as Mrs. Keats – the housekeeper – and who might someday see a picture of Mrs. Ashbury and sound the alarm. Bowles and Spiker, it turns out, were private detectives accompanying the younger Ashburys on their quest to capture their stepmother and return her to where she can be controlled. There is more overt action in this one than usual, and Gamadge even carries a gun.

Night Walk (1947) is another slight variation from Daly's formula. A tiny New England town is troubled one night by a string of incidents involving a prowler who tries to open doors in a rest home, a library, and a rooming house before entering the home of Lawrence and Lidia Carrington – brother and sister – and bludgeoning their father to death in his bed. Also living in the house is Rose Jenner, ward of the dead man. None of these three gain anything from his death and in fact they lose his annuity and will actually be worse off.

Gamadge is brought into the case by Garston Yates, who was staying overnight at the rooming house in rooms belonging to a man named Compson when the prowler appeared. He is clandestinely romancing Rose Jenner. Rose is almost the only character whose alibi is not ironclad, since she was alone at the movies when the prowler struck. All of the others were in groups and it appears that none of them could have been responsible for all the incidents. The suspicious reader will probably conclude at this point that the early incidents were designed to give the impression that the killer is an outsider, while the truth might well be that the dead man was the target right from the outset.

To conduct his investigation, Gamadge poses as a guest at the rest home run by Martine Studley. Gamadge checks the background of the other guests and only a man named Motley lacks a solid background. He also learns that no one knew that Compson had left early on his current trip, so he may have been the target rather than Yates. Motley turns out to be a false name for Matthews, who knows Mrs. Turnbull, another resident at the rest home, and was peripherally involved when her husband committed suicide. He is trying to romance her for her money. Then Miss Bluett, the librarian, is killed in the same manner and that seems to point to a random series of killings. There is evidence that the killer was hiding in the attic of the library. The obvious explanation is that this is more camouflage, but Daly actually provides a motive, though a tenuous one.

Rose has an apparent moment of intuition and asks them to look inside an elaborate trellis attached to their house. They do so and find a cudgel which may have been left behind by the killer. Gamadge and Yates both mention that there is something fishy about her sudden inspiration. Gamadge knows by now who the real killer is and lays a successful trap during which Lawrence Carrington is exposed as the killer.

The motive is never apparent until it is revealed. Both Carrington and his father were in love with Rose, who had already rejected the younger man. When Lawrence discovered that his father was planning to propose, he killed him but failed to recover the letter he was writing. It was inside a book which was donated to the library, and that's why Miss Bluett had to die. The ending isn't entirely satisfactory but it does tie everything up.

The Book of the Lion (1948) starts quietly. Avery Bradlock convinces Gamadge to take a look at his late brother's correspondence, to determine if it has any value. Paul Bradlock was a writer whose career was disappointing despite a promising beginning and who died violently, killed by parties unknown while walking in a park at night. The letters have been collected by Paul's widow, Vera. Avery's wife turns up to apologize for her husband's awkward approach and invites him to dinner. Donald Malcolm and his wife Elena return for an extended cameo because Gamadge consults them about Paul Bradlock. Clara also makes a brief appearance but we still have not actually met Gamadge's son or even learned his name.

Gamadge arrives for dinner only to discover that the letters have already been sold and that he has been invited under false pretenses. He is introduced to Avery's mother-in-law, Mrs. Longridge, and Hill Iverson, the man who is buying the letters. He also meets Sally Orme, Vera Bradlock's cousin, and Sally's friend Tom Welsh.

Gamadge is suspicious of the circumstances surrounding the sale. It all happened too quickly and he suspects that Vera was covering up the fact that she had already sold the correspondence, or that there was no correspondence to sell. Since Avery has been supporting her for years, she would not want him to know that she had had another source of income. Malcolm does some undercover work that pretty much confirms that the box was empty.

Gamadge sets out to track down an old friend of Paul Bradlock, a woman named Isabel Wakes, who appears to have dropped out of sight. He is then invited to meet with Iverson and the widow, who tell him that Paul had found a copy of a lost book by Chaucer and that they sold it to an expert who was lost, along with the manuscript, in a plane crash. Gamadge, unconvinced, goes back to see Wakes a second time and finds her dead in her apartment.

The police think it was a suicide and that Wakes killed Bradlock and feared that Gamadge would discover the truth. Gamadge insists that it was murder, and also tells the police that the story about a lost Chaucer is nonsense. He also suggests that he was told the elaborate story to provide an alibi for the people responsible for Wakes' death.

Once again Daly makes no real secret of the identities of the killers. Vera and Iverson have been blackmailing Mrs. Bradlock because she was involved in a forgery scheme in Paris years earlier. Gamadge manages to get the incriminating letter – which they had taken from Paul Bradlock's body after killing him, and which he in turn had gotten from Wakes. That ends the blackmail and there is a falling out between Iverson and Vera. The former kills the latter and is then killed himself in an encounter with a man working for Gamadge. The ending is rather flat this time because there are no surprises at the end and both of the deaths take place off stage.

And Dangerous to Know (1949) introduces us to the Dunbar family, comfortable if not rich. Angus is the head of the family, along with his wife. They have a daughter Alice who lives with them and a younger daughter, Abigail Tanner, widowed and now back with her parents but only temporarily. She has independent means. They have assembled because of the death of a great aunt, named

Woodworth. Angus is the executor of the estate. There is also a cousin Bruce, who is comparatively poor. Alice does not get along with her family and one day she buys new clothes, changes her appearance, and disappears without a word.

A few weeks later, Gamadge looks into the disappearance and starts by talking to Woodworth's housemaid. Although her death appears to be from natural causes, he is still interested in the last of several men she had been helping find work after the war, the only one of whom the servants never learned his name. He talks to them as well as to Arthur Jennings, whom knew the dead woman as well as socializing with Abigail.

He discovers that Alice never showed up for her regularly scheduled art classes and was obviously meeting someone else on a regular basis. The art teacher followed her one night and gives Gamadge the address of the apartment building she was visiting. She also tells him that Alice expected to inherit the Woodhouse fortune, which was instead left to a hospital.

Pretending to be apartment hunting, Gamadge talks to the neighbors and finds out that the man Alice was visiting was named Fuller, but that he has gone away. He also discovers that Fuller only was accepted as a tenant because of a recommendation from Mrs. Woodworth, suggesting that he was one of her charitable projects and his description matches the man the servants talked about. Fuller said that he was a landscape gardener and he arranged for major renovations to the garden, which suggests that there might be a body buried there. There is, of course, and Alice Dunbar has been found.

Gamadge accepts an invitation to visit the hotel lounge frequented by Abigail and her friends, one of whom is an accomplished singer. He recalls that Woodworth's mysterious protégé was also known for his singing ability. He tries to trick the killer into exposing himself by singing an obscure song, but the trick fails, and then the man is found dead just outside the hotel, and it looks like suicide. The revolver he used is the same one that killed Alice Dunbar. The gun formerly belonged to Abigail's dead husband.

The obvious motive is that the killer was hoping to marry Alice until he discovered she wasn't going to inherit a fortune, then killed her to simplify replacing her with the sister. It is also clear that the dead singer did not commit suicide, that he was killed to give the impression that he was responsible for Alice's death. Daly has a surprise for the reader, however, and the killer turns out to be Bruce Dunbar, who had romanced Alice, then dropped her. Driven over the edge, she had gone to murder him but he had gotten the upper hand. The second half is rather slow at times, but the red herrings are quite well done.

Death and Letters (1950) has another unusual opening. The Coldfield family lives in a secluded mansion and does not welcome guests. Ames Coldfield is the head of the family and his son Ira is married to Georgette. Glendon Colfield, Ira's brother, was married to Sylvia but has recently died. Ira and Georgette have a daughter Susan. Sylvia is being held prisoner in the house, apparently with the assistance of a local doctor, for reasons unknown, but she smuggles out a letter which comes to the attention of Henry Gamadge. The letter requests help and suggests that she is in danger.

Gamadge does some research. Glendon died of an overdose that might have been an accident or self inflicted, but there are suspicions that he might have been helped along. Sylvia almost died a short time later, also an overdose of sedatives, but survived. She denies that she attempted suicide. Gamadge and Bantz successfully liberate/abduct her from the house, but the rest of the Coldfields insist that she is mentally unbalanced even though she appears perfectly normal. She tells Gamadge that she is convinced someone in the family has gone mad and that both poisonings were intentional. When she mentioned this to Ames, she was promptly placed incommunicado in anticipation of having her committed to an asylum.

The motive appears to be the discovery of some valuable but scandalous letters a long deceased grandmother received from a famous poet. Someone discovered their existence and secretly sold them, and Glendon must have learned the truth. Concealing his discovery from the family, Gamadge meets with them to pick up clothing for Sylvia and to reassure them about the situation in order to ameliorate any lingering threat. He concludes that Ames knew about the letters and that someone had sold them, but that he was not personally involved. We are meant to believe that Georgette is responsible, but the introduction of Zelma, the young woman who was formerly involved with Susan's fiancé, undermines the plot slightly. It is obvious that she will get him back, and the only way that can happen is if Susan is eliminated, and thus she has to be the murderer.

Although medical standards have changed, it is hard to credit Daly's explanation that the family doctor really believed that Sylvia should be forcibly restrained indefinitely with no outside contact. It is in fact not even essential to the plot although it does provide the excuse for an exciting rescue sequence. That aside, this is a well constructed puzzle that is undercut slightly by obvious clues about the outcome.

The Book of the Crime (1951) was Daly's last mystery novel. Rena Austen is feeling considerable discontent about her life with husband Gray, who shares a house with his brother and sister, Jerome and Hildreth. Gray was partly disabled during the war, but has enough money to live on, and Rena has no friends in the city and feels isolated and lonely. They married on impulse and she is convinced that neither of them was really in love.

One day she is dusting some books when her husband suddenly flies into a rage, takes the book away, and locks her in her room. She manages to escape with the aid of a neighbor named Ordway and flees into hiding. Gray then attempts to hire Gamadge to track her down. This is ironic because she is secretly staying with Henry and his wife. All that she can tell him about the books in question was that they appeared to be transcripts of some sort of trial. From her description it appears that the books are at least a century old. We also learn from the Ordways that Rena was Gray's second wife. The first was an alcoholic who died of pneumonia.

Gamadge visits the Austen house at Gray's request and hears a very different version of events. On his way home, accompanied briefly by Hildreth, he stumbles across the body of a young man in a nearby alley. Gamadge theorizes that the victim was on his way to blackmail Gray, that Jerome killed him, and Hildreth was supposed to discover the body. The truth begins to come out at that point. The real Gray Austen died a long time before, of natural causes, and another man took his place, sharing the estate income with the surviving siblings. He is arrested, but it is unlikely he knew about the murder – a man who knew the real Gray – until after the fact.

There is a bit of tidying up – the murder has to be proven – and Gamadge explains why the books were so alarming to the impostor. They referred to a fraudulent claim to an estate and, coupled with Rena's comment that he no longer needed her – which he interpreted as her recognition that he was not really lame – he panicked.

The plot this time is very similar to that of the preceding book, the woman in peril and imprisoned by her family, the old secret which could lead to scandal, the wealthy aristocrats whose fortunes have been declining, the clannishness and domination by a single member, and the appeal to Gamadge by a relative stranger. The Gamadges now have a second child, also unnamed, and we don't even learn its sex. This was not her strongest book, but she ended her career on a high note.

Daly only started writing mysteries quite late in life but produced them regularly from that point onward. Gamadge is an interesting character and his profession often provides an interesting twist on his detection. Her weakest books are early ones although even those are generally interesting. The later books often experiment with different types of puzzles and plots. Although she never wrote a specific novel that stood out as a genre classic, her work is generally of quite high quality.

CHARITY BLACKSTOCK

Charity Blackstock was one of three pseudonyms used by British novelist Ursula Torday (1912-1997). Torday wrote mostly historical and contemporary romances, but the Blackstock name was reserved initially for mystery novels, although from the 1960s onward she pretty much abandoned the genre. One American edition changed the name to Lee Blackstock for no apparent reason. Torday wrote over sixty novels during her lifetime and was once nominated for the Edgar Award for best mystery novel.

Her first mystery was *Dewey Death* (1956). Barbara Smith is a librarian who has just sold her first historical romance novel, to be published under a pseudonym she has never revealed to her coworkers. She works for an interlibrary loan center with several young women and Mrs. Warren, an unpleasant older woman who goes out of her way to make herself disagreeable. Other employees include Mark Allan, who feels unrequited love for Mrs. Bridgewater despite her marriage, and Mr. Rills, a habitual troublemaker. There is also Miss Holmes, the immediate supervisor, and Mr. Dodds, who works in an associated capacity. A younger man, Wilson, believes – or at least pretends to believe – that the library is being used to cover a drug smuggling operation.

The tension suddenly grows much more acrimonious. Rills is clearly terrified by something Mrs. Warren has found out and Allan, who was a commando during the war, is clearly enraged by her. Except for Smith, none of the characters are particularly admirable and most are petty, vindictive, egotistical, foolish, or erratic. It is clear from the outset, however, that Mrs. Warren is going to be murdered.

On the crucial day Mr. Latimer, the highest ranking person at the site, finds himself locked in the lavatory when the mechanism jams. This causes a minor sensation and people are generally away from the places where they usually work during the confusion. After the confusion has subsided, it is discovered that Mrs. Warren has gone missing. The time involved is just over half an hour.

A number of people are acting strangely. Mrs. Bridgewater bursts into tears, and she has a small cut on one hand. Greta, a teenager, is also in tears following an apparent rebuff by Allan, for whom she has a crush. She mentions that his hands were dripping wet, ostensibly because he was developing some photostats. He seems remarkably angry, as does Mr. Purley, the custodian, and Miss Holmes. Even the normally calm Mr. Dodds suggests that the missing woman deserved to be murdered. It is no surprise therefore when Warren's body is found in a sack used for carrying large quantities of books about. Someone has broken her neck.

The description of police procedure is superficial and a bit questionable. None of the staff are interviewed on the day of the crime, not even Smith, who discovered the body. They are allowed to go home but are told that they will be questioned at work the following day.

Most of the women are interviewed together because the police believe that they would not have been physically capable of the crime. Unlike most mystery novelists who would have reproduced large portions of each interview, Blackstock summarizes this in a single paragraph. The police are told by Latimer that they have recently discovered that several of the rare books they store on site have disappeared, presumably stolen, and that an investigation is ongoing. The thefts took place over a period of eighteen months, and since only Wilson is a new hire, all of the staff are potential suspects.

Smith, who writes romantic novels and has a very nice journalist named Charles for a boyfriend, is nevertheless attracted to Allan despite his bad temper. Bridgwater has broken off her flirtation with Allan, much to his chagrin, and begins to make advances to Wilson despite the disparity in their ages. Tension builds dramatically as Smith breaks off her engagement to Charles, Wilson has an argument with Allan, and Bridgwater retreats into an uneasy and prolonged silence.

The individual interviews provider a few tidbits. Bridgwater contradicts herself about the cut on her hand, but it was obvious from the outset that she was lying about it. Allan interprets her erratic behavior as evidence that she saw something the day of the murder which she is keeping to herself. Wilson unwisely announces that he is on the trail of dangerous criminals using the library, but then refuses to say anything to the police out of fear of being made to look ridiculous.

Allan finds some paperwork suggesting that Rills was deeply in debt and his behavior during the interview suggests that he was responsible for the missing books. Dodds tells Smith that he knows who the killer is but that he has no proof. The pot simmers for awhile with little activity by the police but considerable tension among the characters.

A small crisis develops because of some misdirected mail, during the course of which Blackstock provides some foreshadowing, suggesting that Wilson is accompanied by the figure of death itself. Smith struggles with her feelings for Allan, whose moments of good humor are overshadowed by his tendency to be rude, overbearing, and a bully. There is also a hint that the police believe that Allan is the killer.

Wilson sneaks into an unspecified office and takes an unidentified object from the desk. This appears to be the crucial clue in his investigation and he takes the elevator down to the deserted stacks to examine it. Unfortunately, he was not unobserved and the killer follows. Wilson is fatally struck, but the object rolls under a shelf and the murderer does not find it. Allan is not at work that day, but of course that doesn't mean he wasn't in the building. The police, however, have been following him but lost him during the critical time.

The foreshadowing this time is fairly explicit. The announcement by the police that there will be no more murders is characterized as "over-optimistic," although they prove to be correct. Bridgewater confesses that she saw Mrs. Warren's body in the bag, but insists that Dodds must have been the killer. She cut her hand when she was retying the bag. But the police have traced clandestine payments into Allan's bank account and it is fairly obvious that the drugs have been concealed in microfilm containers. They close in but Allan commits suicide by jumping from this office window.

Although superficially structured as a conventional detective story, Dewey Death is unusual in several small but distinct ways. There is no real detective, official or amateur. Although there is a very narrow timeframe for the first murder, there is no effort to chart the activities of the various characters or to determine whether or not they had alibis. There is no physical evidence. The interviews are perfunctory or truncated. The interactions among the characters are the chief focus of the plot, and for the most part they do not directly involve the murder. The solution is also unusual in that the person most likely to be the murderer is in fact guilty, and the police know it well in advance of the final scenes.

The characterization is impressively detailed, even for the minor characters. It is difficult, however, to identify with Smith who consistently makes bad choices even in the presence of overwhelming evidence that she is making a mistake. There is a good deal of tension, but not much mystery since it is so obvious so early that Allan is the villain.

Next came *The Woman in the Woods* (aka *Miss Fenny*) which appeared in 1957, which was a nominee for the Edgar Award. Some boys playing in the woods stumble upon human bones in the opening scene. The body is that of a woman and she has clearly been buried a long time before a violent storm undercut the ground and exposed her to view. Tim Brennan, their teacher, reluctantly but almost immediately concludes that it was murder.

The reader is then introduced to various residents of the local village. Dr. Heslop is the physician. Mr. Plumtree is a mildly reclusive novelist. Miss Brooks fancies herself a painter. Lady Grail is the local aristocrat, used to having things her way. Her husband is Sir Malcolm. Nicole Sherratt is a local woman and a widow whose eight year old son Daniel is confined to bed, more or less permanently. The doctor is pursuing Sherratt romantically, although he has an unofficial girlfriend named Rose, his receptionist. Brennan is also wooing the widow. Sergeant Hawkes is the village policeman and Mike Lord is the bright teenager who discovered the body.

We are able to eliminate a few characters as suspects almost immediately. The discovery is made from Brennan's viewpoint and he is clearly surprised. The opening set of relationships makes it likely that he is going to end up with Sherratt, although Blackstock's first novel has warned us that she doesn't always provide a happy ending. Hawkes seems too enthusiastic about having a murder to investigate to be guilty. Heslop, on the other hand, is egocentric and prone to fits of rage which is reminiscent of Allan, the murderer in *Dewey Death*. Plumtree is vindictive and nosey.

Since Daniel is bedridden but has a window, he sees much more that is going on in the village than does anyone else. He also has an imaginary friend – Miss Fenny – through whose agency he appears to glean even more knowledge. Daniel claims that she visits him regularly and that she is angry with an unidentified man who hurt her sister.

The body is approximately a year old and since no one is missing from the village, it is assumed that the victim was someone passing through the area. Our first hint of her identity is when Brennan reminisces about his brief sexual encounter with Queenie Holroyd, a onetime vaudeville actress whom he approached after being rebuffed by Sherratt early in their relationship. Her description is also close to that of Miss Fenny provided by Daniel, so Blackstock probably intended for us to believe that this was the injured sister.

Blackstock reveals part of the truth very early. After examining the body, Heslop returns to his home in a foul mood and through his thoughts we learn that he knows who the woman was, knows she had a sister, and it is probably he who killed and buried her. The mystery in this case will not be the identity of the murderer or the method by which it was done, but rather the chain of events which will lead to his downfall.

Our viewpoint switches to Daniel for a while and his memories confirm that Miss Fenny and Queenie are the same person. Mike Lord confides to Brennan that he saw Heslop have a tantrum and that he believes the doctor is the murderer. It develops that most of the other characters knew and liked Queenie, even Plumtree thinks of her fondly and mentions that her sister died of an overdose of medication during an abortion. It is in fact a bit puzzling at this point that no one connected Queenie with the bones, given that the woman disappeared mysteriously at just the right time.

Heslop begins to lose control. He strikes Rose for no particular reason and then explodes at Miss Brooks, humiliating her. The noose tightens when a distraught Rose tells Plumtree that she found a distinctive bra in the doctor's office a year earlier, and Plumtree knows that the bra belonged to Queenie. He confronts Heslop and drops hints that he knows the doctor murdered her, and that same day the police identify the remains as expected.

When Heslop realizes that Plumtree knows the truth, he pushes him off a bridge but, quite by chance, the fall is cut short and Brennan later rescues him. There is a mild flaw here. Plumtree has not gone to the police because they have always terrified him, which is vaguely possible, but neither will he confide in Brennan, which seems completely illogical under the circumstances, particularly since he has just confirmed that he was pushed off the bridge. Daniel repeats some of the things Queenie told him a year earlier and that provokes Heslop into planning another murder – but he is still unaware of the fact that Plumtree has survived. When a storm knocks out all the telephones, he decides the time has come to act.

Mike Lord knows that Heslop is planning to murder Daniel, but not only are the phones out but Brennan has gone off with Sherratt for a picnic and the village constable is out of town. This is the ultimate decision point for the Brennan/Sherratt connection. She reveals herself to be a petty, death obsessed snob and he finally decides that they could never be happy together. This all changes after he prevents Heslop from killing Daniel, thanks to Mike Lord, and the story ends with them engaged and Heslop under arrest.

Blackstock's prose is vivid with imagery and allusion. There is a particularly effective passage when Brennan predicts that the discovery of the body will affect the lives of everyone in the village. "And this, make no mistake, is our Armageddon. We have unleashed the ghosts…" She does repeat things from the first book – the irritable characters are very similar, and Mike Lord's secretive quest to prove that the doctor is the killer resembles Wilson's efforts to unmask the drug ring. Sherratt is emotionally volatile as was Miss Smith and the inquisitive and vaguely repulsive Plumtree is a slightly more composed version of Mr. Rills.

There is rather a lot of coincidence. Plumtree knew Queenie as a child when they lived near one another elsewhere in England, and Brennan is not only from the same place but lived in the same house, though not at the same time. As with the first novel, the police investigation all takes place off stage. There is a strong hint of the supernatural in this one. Brennan thinks he sees Queenie in Daniel's room, and both he and Sherratt hear her voice at crucial moments. Supernatural elements are not always compatible with mystery novels, but in this case it fits the mood of the story.

The Foggy, Foggy Dew (1958) opens with Andrew Mallory, a scientist who spends much of his time on a Pacific island studying the natives, accepting an invitation to visit Jim and Mary Cakebread. Mary is an old friend. Jim works in the British colonial office. Andrew is rather depressed, in large part because of the deteriorating international situation in Europe and in part because of the isolation of his lifestyle. The heavy fog in London on the night of the party exacerbates his mood. Andrew and Mary were once romantically involved, but it is long over by this time.

Mallory is cut from a familiar mold. Although his excuse is that he is drunk, he is pointlessly rude to a very young woman he meets at the party. He later apologizes and offers to escort her during a walk to a local nightclub. In the interim he has had a brief encounter with an unpleasant man named Gerald and learned that the young woman is one of Jim's clerks. There is significant foreshadowing at this point, with several remarks about Mallory remembering certain details of her dress later on.

The nightclub is packed and Mallory spots an enigmatic woman whose appearance fascinates him. As part of the show, the master of ceremonies issues a supposed message from Queen Victoria to the inhabitants of the very island where he has been conducting his research, even though she is long dead. Impulsively the young girl announces that the two of them are from the island, causing a mild stir, and Mallory suddenly senses that there is great danger hovering about them. The message is a cryptic reference to fifty children.

The young woman, whose name we still do not know, never returns from the restrooms. Convinced that something is wrong, Mallory enters and finds her dead in one of the stalls, struck from behind. He doesn't tell anyone and impulsively takes her brooch with him and leaves the nightclub. That night, he wakens in his room to find the strange woman from the nightclub has broken in. She identifies herself as Emmi, admits to coming from the continent, but initially refuses to cooperate otherwise other than to confirm that she was supposed to kill him but couldn't bring herself to do it.

Eventually she tells him that the fifty children are important refugees and that the nightclub was the means of delivering a message so that someone could prevent their escape. She believes that her employers have already killed her own parents and husband and that they are set upon Mallory's death as well. Having told him this much, she cannot return to her masters – transparently communists - and he refuses to turn her over to the police.

Blackstock's ambivalence about her major characters is apparent here, and both are deeply flawed. Despite his crudeness and bad temper, Mallory is committed to rescuing the children, but not for their sake. Rather, he intends to avenge the young girl who was needlessly murdered. Emmi, despite her qualms about killing Mallory, considers the dead girl a worthless nonentity not worth the effort and later characterizes the older people in the refugee camps as useless. Mallory also begins to suspect that she is not really committed to finding the children.

Mallory finds a sleazy criminal among the refugees who offers to sell him the information he is looking for, but when Mallory arrives at the rendezvous, he discovers that the man has been murdered. He neither reports this to the police nor tells Emmi what has happened. They travel to the refugee camps on the continent but when they find someone who may know about the children, he is murdered before they can question him. And then Mallory is kidnapped and beaten by men led by the mysterious Englishman he saw at the party where everything started. They are convinced that he knows where the children are.

Mallory escapes by letting gas escape into the house when they think he is unconscious. Emmi shows up to rescue him or he would have died with his captors. But he begins to realize the truth. Despite her feelings for him, she is still working for the foreign agents. She is the one who killed the young girl, and the man on the continent as well. She was using him to search for the children. He takes her mountain climbing and more or less arranges for her to have a fatal accident.

Despite a very good opening, this novel bogs down considerably by the halfway point. The plot flounders around making no headway and the characters – particularly Mallory – are prone to making very long speeches which are often repetitive and rarely realistic. Mallory finds an important clue after speaking to only two refugees in Europe, which also seems unlikely given the great secrecy surrounding the children. Emmi's continued cooperation with the communists is evident quite early and only Mallory's means of dealing with the problem is at all surprising.

When *All Men Are Murderers* (1958) appeared in the US, the title was changed to *The Shadow of Murder* and the byline to Lee Blackstock. Johnny Shawfield is spending some time in Scotland to get over his recent divorce from Sylvia Court, a popular actress. Within the first two pages the reader knows that this is another of Blackstock's short tempered, egocentric male protagonists. Even a clerk refers to him in those terms and later he recalls having started to strangle his wife.

He meets Kate Stewart and her mother en route and she tells him that the remote hotel where he'll be staying currently has only two other residents. One is Ian Macdonald, who is doing research about local history for a book in progress. The other is Curtis, a retired banker who recently suffered a nervous breakdown. He also learns that there are rumors that a fugitive wife killer named Lionel Merritt is hiding in the area. Arriving at the hotel he meets Mrs. Forbes, the manager, and Hughie, a horse that has become something of a shared local pet.

Curtis seems innocuous but Macdonald is rude and excitable and there is immediate tension between them. Forbes tells Shawfield that the Stewarts are about to lose their farm. Shawfield talks to Kate and they discover that they both feel some sympathy for the fugitive. Macdonald shows him an antique pistol, which he has foolishly loaded, and the weapon subsequently disappears briefly.

The eviction takes place and Kate takes refuge in the hotel because a blizzard is about to close the pass and maroon them. Her mother has supposedly gone to stay with a sister in Edinburgh. They are remote enough that the hotel doesn't even have a telephone. Tensions build as the relationships among the characters are constantly changing. There are hints that the murderer is actually either Macdonald or Curtis, as unlikely as it seems.

The emotions and tensions finally reach a climax and the shadow of the fugitive murderer hangs over them all. The killer has a distinctive cut on one wrist, and Shawfield inadvertently imitates himself in a similar fashion. By chance, he goes to a movie and it features his ex-wife. During the course of the film he decides to return to London and kill her, and Kate instinctively realizes what he is thinking. When she tries to convince him to drop his plan, he strikes her in the face and any lingering sympathy by the reader is promptly exorcised.

Shawfield decides to walk to the next town and make his way out of Scotland, but Macdonald tries to kill him with his two shot antique pistol. The first shot misses and the second chamber proves to be empty. It was used earlier to kill Kate's mother, who is lying buried in the snow. The killer is obviously Curtis, who is also the fugitive, although the author never explains why the police have not been around given that they believe him to be staying in a hotel. Curtis, who is clearly insane, killed Stewart because she was cruel to animals. When Shawfield confronts him he tries to get away in his car and goes off a cliff.

Although Blackstock varies her plots considerably, she seemed to have gotten into a rut with her characters and their interactions. The male lead is constantly apologizing for his rudeness and cruelty, but never makes any real effort to stop acting that way. Shawfield considers it a "gross injustice" when Kate accuses him of being the main cause of the turmoil at the hotel, but she is undeniably correct. The supporting male characters are generally socially inept cowards. Kate is more decisive than the earlier female leads, and in many ways more competent as well, but even she is prone to occasional lapses from character, though she is perhaps the first to be more pleasant than otherwise. Many of her characters know what they should do in emotional situations, buy they always lack the courage to act appropriately.

Witches' Sabbath (1961) was originally published as by Paula Allardyce. It won the Romantic Novel of the Year award. Tamar Brown is a writer specializing in occult subjects who travels to a remote English town named Meadway Bois to do research concerning Abigail Parkes, executed as a witch centuries earlier. By chance, she bears a passing physical resemblance to the descriptions of the supposed witch. She is no longer romantically attached to William, yet another young man subject to violent rages. William, a doctor, has married Margaret instead.

Upon arriving she immediately meets Humphrey Sloane, an artist living in the cottage once owned by Parkes, who characterizes himself as the town scandal, primarily because he's an outsider and the insular villagers, he insists, still believe in witchcraft. The other villagers are a varied lot. Mrs. Belling, whose quiet husband occasionally grows violent when he has been drinking, is the town gossip and telephone operator, and she listens in on her calls. The local pub is owned by Mr. and Mrs. Parsons. Mrs. Parsons believes that Parkes was a real witch and resents the visitor, as do several others. Dr. Randall, the doctor, is also viewed askance because he is an outsider. His wife recently died and his sister Ruth lives with him. The vicar, Kingham, is an elderly widower and has a grown daughter, Doreen. Ann Leigh, the local unwed mother, is a descendant of one of the alleged victims of Parkes, who supposedly cursed her baby.

Sloane proves to be another chauvinistic male character when he alleges that women enjoy being physically mistreated. Dr. Randall is also notoriously bad tempered, Belling is murderous when drunk and, through flashbacks, we learn that William was also short tempered and abusive. Randall asserts that "She just lets her emotions rule her. Like all women." One might wonder what kind of men the author knew personally. The vicar tells her that he thinks she is ill advised in choosing Parkes as her subject matter and even Brown herself experiences a vague feeling that she is disturbing things best left alone. The characters in general are superstitious and bellicose, even those with no reason to be that way.

Blackstock invokes a contrived coincidence at this point. Dr. Randall is in fact William, whom she hasn't seen for six years. After Margaret's death, he changed his name. When she tells him how much she has resented the ill mannered way that he treated her, he insists that she apologize for being rude and she does so. Blackstock's female characters are almost invariably either harridans or overly submissive.

Tension builds slowly. Tom Belling decides that Brown is a witch. Sloane brings her a cat because he thinks she should have a "familiar." It seems magical to some that both Sloane and the reclusive Dr. Randall have both apparently fallen for the newcomer in a matter of hours. Randall's sister, who detests Brown, claims to be psychic and starts to spread rumors about witchcraft. The local legend is that the witch's ashes were buried in a metal box, and that if the box is ever opened, Parkes will return in a new body. This is a not very subtle foreshadowing of what is to come.

Ruth tells Brown that Margaret committed suicide in an attempt to drive a wedge between her and William. She then tells her brother that Brown wormed the information out of her. The scene that follows is, alas, completely implausible. Even though Randall has finally realized that their initial quarrel was the result of Ruth having lied to him, and even though he has just warned Brown that Ruth will do anything to keep them apart, he assumes that she has told him the truth and abusively confronts Brown demanding an explanation. And just as before, Brown is too angry to tell him the truth, even though she pleads with him not to be angry with her. Even if this was remotely plausible it would render both characters so unsympathetic that the reader would no longer by capable of identifying with them.

Meanwhile, Anne Leigh's most recent child, a baby, contracts measles and she refuses to follow the doctor's instructions, preferring wards against deviltry to actual medicine. This echoes the crime Parkes was accused of, and the parallel is emphasized because Brown has named her cat after the one owned by the alleged witch. Brown agrees to Ruth's suggestion that she tie flowers to the Leigh's front gate, which is even more implausible than the confrontation with Randall. For someone who is supposedly writing a book about historical witchcraft, Brown seems spectacularly uninformed about her subject matter. Sloane even challenges her on this point.

The baby dies and everyone blames Brown. Ruth leaves her alone in William's study, makes a point of telling her where the clippings about the suicide are kept, and Brown gives in to temptation and looks at them. Predictably he was accused of murdering his wife but was found innocent. Naturally he walks in on her while she is reading them. He physically assaults her but apparently Blackstock thinks this is okay because of the circumstances since Brown immediately forgives him.

As the reader has expected for some time, the following day opens with the discover that someone has dug up and removed Parkes' remains. It is obvious that Sloane is responsible, which is confirmed when Belling – who had passed out near the grave – hints that he saw the whole thing. Ruth, who is obviously insane, admits to having murdered Margaret, and has also set fire to the schoolhouse where Brown is working on her notes. William rescues her and Ruth dies in the fire.

The plot this time is appallingly bad. The structure is only maintained by people acting against their own best interests, withholding information needlessly, not heeding obvious warnings or learning from their mistakes, plus coincidences to put all the proper pieces into play. The characters act so badly – even Brown – that their supposed redeeming qualities are quite overwhelmed. Brown is supposed to be a competent researcher, but she lacks even rudimentary knowledge about her subject. William's secretiveness is disproportionate to the circumstances. Doreen is another of Blackstock's infuriatingly submissive females and Sloane is another of her whining, abusive, and chauvinistic young males. The US paperback edition labeled this as a "Black Magic Novel of Terror" but there is little suspense, let alone terror, and no magic at all, black or otherwise.

A House Possessed (1961) was also published as *The Exorcism*. Mrs. Murphy inherited a large house in which she rents rooms. The house is filled with curios, some of them moderately valuable, but the best of all is the only one actually kept locked up, a piece of jewelry that once belonged to Mary, Queen of Scots. The house is famously haunted by the ghost of a woman who lost her husband during the Napoleonic Wars but Mrs.Murphy decides to have a local priest exorcize the spirit. There is also supposed to be a secret passage, but no one has ever figured out where it is.

Peter Haynes, a young boy who lives there, has a habit of wandering around in the dark and he notices that another resident, Mr. Ingham, quietly does the same. Ingham, an American, has very poor manners. Peter seems to know a great many details about the history of the ghost which no one seems to have told him. Peter lives with his father, Nigel, and his aunt, Barbara, who do not like each other. Other residents include Miss Leslie, is a social worker, and Flight Sergeant Major, who has mental problems and has a mild case of paranoia. Ingham is a newcomer but years earlier he and Barbara had had an unhappy love affair. Neither of them are prepared to meet again under these circumstances.

Ingham, our romantic lead, is another man who is bad tempered, and who is convinced that women enjoy his lack of manners. His earlier meeting with Barbara is revealed through a series of flashbacks so it is not until quite late in the story that we understand the circumstances of their parting. Even then there were abusive elements in their relationship. On their last day together in Greece, he promised to meet her and never showed up, and she never heard from him again. She attributes this to her unwillingness to have sexual relations with him on the previous day.

As the time for the exorcism approaches, tempers begin to fray for a variety of reasons. Miss Leslie intrudes into the private life of one of the staff members and is rebuffed, after which she takes out her anger on Peter, who swears mildly in response. This is reported to his father, whose rigid self control slips, and Barbara suddenly recognizes the absurdity of the situation and bursts out laughing, which offends him even further. In the hours before the exorcism is to start, the strange sounds which are associated with the ghost become more common and even Barbara believes that she has heard the ghostly girl and her lover speaking to one another.

Nigel gets drunk and provokes a fight with Ingham, which echoes a confrontation in the story of the ghostly couple. Miss Leslie, contrite about her overreaction to Peter, turns out to be a better person than she seemed. She prevents Major from committing suicide and feels genuine sympathy for him. The priest, meanwhile, finds himself dealing with a throng of spirits, real or within his mind. Blackstock invokes another of her stock situations at this point. Barbara misapprehends when she finds a female servant in Ingham's room but rather than seek an explanation, she draws hasty, inaccurate, and rather silly conclusions.

Barbara then catches Ingham when he is about to steal the valuable jewelry and replace it with a fake. In his own word, Ingham is "not a very nice character." He was stealing out of boredom as much as a desire for money. He tells her that he disappeared from her life ten years earlier because he was afraid of getting tied up in a permanent relationship. This supposedly somehow excuses his actions in not at least telling her what had happened.

The exorcism is completed and the priest leaves but the sound of crying suddenly permeates the house. Ingham finds the secret passage with remarkable ease and inside is Peter, who is responsible for the strange sounds and has been all along. He also found the diary of the supposed ghost, which explains how he knew things that no one had told him about the history of her tragic death. Even Nigel seems somewhat transformed, repentant about the way he talked to both Ingham and Barbara while he was drunk. Everyone seems to have become at least minimally a better person as a consequence of the events at the lodge.

There are some slight variations in Blackstock's narrative technique. She repeats particular scenes so that we see events from different points of view. Otherwise this follows her usual pattern. Once again her female characters are generally silly or malevolent, or both other than Barbara who is another submissive woman who doesn't mind her lover's mistreatment. Ingham, like Brennnan in *The Woman in the Woods*, likes children and is always kind to them, but needlessly and with fair consistency mistreats even the woman he loves. The two protagonists do not end up together at the end, although they tentatively agree to see each other back in London, although it seems likely this will not happen.

Her next novel was *The Gallant* (1962). Ross MacLeod is hired by Sir Arthur Haley-Whyte, whose wealth is based on his magazine publishing business. Ross has recently been divorced after a short marriage that interrupted his college career. Sir Arthur's adult daughter Alice – who is independently wealthy – has run off with Raoul Lestrange, whom Sir Arthur believes is not only after Alice's money but may well murder her once they are married following a three week waiting period in France. He wants Ross to bring Alice back before that happens. There is also a hint that he wouldn't mind if Ross quietly killed Lestrange. Ross is not happy with the job but he needs the money and agrees.

En route, Ross encounters an impressive French businessman named Manade Cesar and later an Englishwoman in a shop whose name he doesn't learn until later. He checks into his hotel – the same one where Alice is staying; Raoul has discreetly taken a room elsewhere. Madame Nicolas, who runs the hotel, apparently knows more about his business than she should. Alice has been told by her father that Ross is coming, and his purpose is not a secret either. Madame Nicolas admits that she thinks Raoul is a fortune hunter, but a charming one.

Cesar tells Ross that his wife has left him for another man, and the description sounds a lot like Raoul. When he finally meets Alice, he recognizes her as the woman he encountered in the shop earlier. At this point he still hasn't seen Raoul, and neither has her father. Alice tells him that Raoul is going to be traveling – he supposedly distributers wines - for the next week. She adamantly refuses to introduce him to either Ross or her father and his mysterious absence all the time would raise the possibility that he does not exist at all if so many people had not been affected by his activities. Alice goes out of her way to mention that he doesn't like having his picture taken. Even Ross muses: "You're not fighting a man. You're fighting a dream."

The only clue about Raoul that Ross possesses is the clipping of a letter published in a French newspaper from a woman seeking male companionship. It was previously in Raoul's wallet. Ross traces the woman – Violette Manchon – and tries to visit her. She is out, but her mother is home and mentions that her daughter is engaged to be married to a wine seller named Raoul Duclos. He also notices that someone is living in a boarded up manor house in the vicinity of the hotel.

Madame Nicolas tells Ross that she has seen Raoul at a nearby hotel even though he is supposedly up in northern France. An American woman whom Ross met briefly on the trip over shows up and announces that she has a new boyfriend. Raoul must have incredible stamina if he is the same man, whom she knows as Roger Thierry. Stymied, Ross is considerably returning to England and abandoning his quest, but oddly, Alice is very upset at the prospect of his leaving. Since Ross has by this point fallen in love with her, this poses emotional problems for him as well.

Ross is also puzzled by Madame Nicolas' senile father, who insists that another Englishman visited him recently. The reader will at this point likely have concluded that the various characters are all actors, hired by Alice's father, and that Raoul in all his various versions is completely imaginary. Ross, however, traces a piece of mail sent to Raoul to an address in England and finds the home Mr. & Mrs. Robert Strange, clearly another manifestation of the same man, and with proof that there is a wife, he is convinced he can talk Alice into changing her plans.

Back in France, Alice tells Ross that she has accepted his arguments and wants to have a confrontation with Raoul at a rendezvous he has provided, which happens to be the boarded up house Ross noticed earlier. Blackstock then reveals that we have been led along a false path. Raoul is real and in fact Ross finds his dead body inside the house. Rather than subject her to the gory scene, he tells Alice that no one was there. Back in England he realizes that Sir Arthur was the killer when he spots an antique watch on his desk that he had previously noticed in a shop near the crime scene.

Blackstock has largely abandoned her stock characters this time around. Ross has a mild temper, but he is neither abusive nor aggressive. Nor is Alice submissive. She stands up to both Ross and her father. Even the supporting characters show some individuality and unpredictability. The story is designed to mislead by keeping Raoul off stage but not so obviously that the reader is likely to realize that the author is playing a game with our perceptions. This was arguably the best of her mystery novels even though the murder doesn't occur until very late in the story.

Mr. Christopoulos (1963) moves further away from mysteries and toward political thriller. Tom Raven is a reporter who was brutalized during the Cyprus civil war. The man who was responsible, Andreas Christopoulos, is now a minister in the government of Cyprus. Naomi Katz is a medical researcher currently assigned to the island. She is being wooed, and not very successfully, by Hugh Kenton. The head of the mission, Lawrence, has invited Christopoulos to a reception even though his past is generally known, but since he is now Minister of Information it is assumed that all is forgiven.

Dick Morgan is the center's security officer and his wife Gwyneth is a not particularly bright woman who looks upon Raven as something of a celebrity and is thrilled that he too is coming to the reception. Other staff includes Jed Carron, the Transport Officer, Dr. Marsh, Director Lawrence, and Sister Christine Campbell. Stavros, a Cypriot, is another of the researchers. The British staff all look down on the locals and Stavros is aware of this fact. As much as he dislikes them in return, he hates Christopoulos even more.

Raven has a preliminary interview with Christopoulos during which he makes sure that he has been recognized. During their earlier encounter, Raven had been mistaken for a spy. He would have died at the man's hands if an unknown woman had not interceded and helped him to escape.

There is sexual as well as political tension among the staff. Raven and Katz spend a night together even though they don't get along very well. Raven becomes increasing ambivalent about the article he is supposed to write, which was meant by his superiors to be complimentary.

The evening of the party arrives. Raven does not attend and Christopoulos is quickly bored and leaves early. Stavros was planning to assassinate him when his car drove past but another driver accidentally ran him down and he dies instead. The security officer covers up the fact that he was undoubtedly planning a murder and the various conflicts wind down to a rather disappointing ending.

There had been hints of the author's revulsion toward the British colonial system in the earlier books, but there is no mistaking it here. Most of the characters use racial slurs constantly and even those who reject racism tend to be condescending and patronizing. She also takes a jab at people who are willing to be tolerant of men they know are monsters. Two staff members who lost a friend to Christopoulos admit that they will have to shake hands with him because it is part of their job. Much of the novel consists of flashbacks to Raven's captivity, torture, escape, and subsequent departure from the island. The exchange between Raven and Stavros about the impracticality of exposing Christopoulos is particularly moving. On the other hand, the sexual antics and jealousies – which are compressed into a very short period of time – seem forced and unrealistic.

The English Wife (1964, aka *The Factor's Wife*) was not packaged as a mystery. It takes place in the early part of the 18th Century. Meg Kerr is devastated when her husband Ringan is accused of murdering several older people. The trial is in the opening scenes, which are followed to a lengthy flashback to 1805 when the two of them first met and fell in love. It then moves back forward to a year before the trial to relate the incidents surrounding the murders.

One of the acquaintances of the couple is named Salie, a roguish sort with a questionable reputation. We already know that he will be chief witness against Ringan at the murder trial. One day Meg witnesses the brutal killing of an old woman and is briefly attacked herself before the murderer flees. She discovers that a program is underway to relocate the small farmers as part of a complicated plan to allow the English to graze their cattle in Scotland, and that sometimes people are killed for resisting. She also discovers that her husband is considered an agent of the English and is therefore thoroughly hated. Ringan assures her that the killer, one of his agents, was drunk at the time and will be punished.

The final section involves the outcome of the trial. There is sufficient evidence that Ringan is exonerated, much to the chagrin of Salie, who turns out to have had an overly simple concept of how the law worked. Although the elements of a traditional mystery are superimposed on the plot, it is largely a historical romance with some mildly suspenseful scenes.

Monkey on a Chain (1965) has also been published as *When the Sun Goes Down*. It is a novel of international intrigue with just a hint of mystery. Sue Douglas had a twin brother who was killed in Southeast Asia during World War II. She learns the name of his killer and finds his present address in Bangkok. Obsessed with confronting him, she leaves her family to travel there. Clancy Fraser was a prisoner of war with her brother John and reportedly he accidentally killed him in 1944. Sue wants to know the full story, despite her husband's objections to her trip.

A good deal of the story consists of flashbacks to how Sue met her husband, who is also a war veteran, and their marriage and life together, and others in which we see her relationship with her twin. When she arrives in Bangkok, she learns that Fraser is away on business and will be gone for three days. On the day of his return, she goes to the office of the newspaper where he is employed as a journalist, only to discover that he is spending the day reporting on a boxing tournament nearby. She searches there and then near a brothel before finally locating him.

To her dismay, he doesn't react to her brother's name and thinks she is just there to visit his grave. He is coarse, rude, and overbearing, but she finds herself becoming attracted to him and decides that she never really loved her husband. She also realizes that her husband opposed her coming because he didn't want her to find out that her brother was not a very nice person, that he provoked the fight in which he was killed by Clancy. She never tells Clancy the truth and decides to return to her family. The mystery has been resolved, but not in the fashion that she had expected. This is a mystery novel by courtesy only.

The Knock at Midnight (1966) is set in 1938, just before the beginning of World War II. Margaret Ramsay's father has recently died and she is feeling somewhat disoriented. She works for an agency which is helping Jewish refugees to escape Nazi Germany and find refuge with relatives in Great Britain and elsewhere. Her father leaves her the bulk of his estate because she was the only one of his three children to help him through his failing years, much to the chagrin of her siblings and their spouses

Maggie announces that she is going to take a vacation in Hungary, and that leads to speculation that she is looking for an old romantic interest, Rupert Cash. She finds him while traveling in Budapest but is appalled to discover that he has apparently become a pro-fascist racist. She also meets some Jewish refugees and feels their plight even more than she did at her desk in England.

There is a murder and it doesn't take long for Maggie to realize that Rupert is the killer. She finds the courage to avenge the woman's death and finds true love with another man in the process. The mystery element comes late in the book and is resolved fairly quickly and with a predictable ending. Although the bones of a mystery story are here, it is clear that Blackstock's interests were now in telling an entirely different kind of story. Blackstock herself worked with refugee children in real life, so that part of the story resonates particularly well.

It would be more than a decade before Blackstock wrote another marginal crime novel. *I Met Murder on the Way* (1977) appeared in the US as *The Shirt Front*. It is essentially a variation of The Knock at Midnight. Victoria Katona is unhappy with her life and is swept up by the charming Zoltan Halasz, who promises to bring her to a safe refuge where she will be safe from the ravages of the world war erupting around her. She discovers fairly quickly that he is actually an Aryan supremacist. There is a murder but it isn't much of a mystery who was responsible.

Blackstock had all the skills to have become a first class mystery writer. Unfortunately she seems to have felt less inclined in that direction – or perhaps her other books sold too well for her to ignore. Even those cases which are more conventional are grudgingly so. She never had a detective as a character, and the police are always window dressing. The emphasis is on character interaction and occasionally suspense, and rarely on clues or elaborate methods. Although she did begin to vary her characters in the later books, the early ones fit into very clear patterns and her protagonists are almost indistinguishable from one book to the next.

INDEX OF TITLES

"1666 and All That" (40)
After Effects (32)
Agony Column, The (89)
All Men Are Murderers (143)
Amendment of Life (34)
And Dangerous to Know (131)
Angel Death (80)
Any Shape or Form (124)
Arrow Pointing Nowhere (121)
"Bare Essentials" (32)
Behind That Curtain (99)
"Benchmark" (40)
Black Camel, The (101)
Black Girl, White Girl (83)
Black Widower (70)
"Blue Upright" (32)
Body Politic, The (29)
Book of the Crime, The (134)
Book of the Dead, The (123)
Book of the Lion, The (130)
"Business Plan" (41)
"Care Plan" (40)
"Cause and Effects" (32)
"Change of Heart, A" (34)
"Chapter and Hearse" (40)
Chapter and Hearse (34)
Charlie Chan Carries On (104)
"Child's Play" (36)
Chinese Parrot, The (96)
Coconut Killings, The (72)
"Cold Comfort" (36)
"Coup de Grace" (36)
Curious Affair of the Third Dog, The (68)
Dead Heading (39)

"Dead Letters" (36)
Dead Liberty, A (28)
Deadly Nightshade (112)
Dead Men Don't Ski (42)
"Deaf Man Talking" (40)
Death and Letters (133)
Death and the Dutch Uncle (61)
Death on the Agenda (49)
"Devilled Dip" (32)
Dewey Death (136)
"Different Cast of Mind, A" (36)
Dollar Chasers, The (91)
"Double Jeopardy" (31)
Down Among the Dead Men (46)
"Due Diligence" (36)
"Dummy Run" (36)
"End Matter" (41)
English Wife, The (153)
"Examination Results" (36)
Evidence of Things Seen (120)
"Exit Strategy" (36)
Exorcism, The (148)
Factor's Wife, The (153)
Falling Star (53)
"Fair Cop, A" (31)
Fifty Candles (90)
Foggy, Foggy Dew, The (141)
Gallant, The (149)
Going Concern, A (30)
"Going Quietly" (40)
"Gold, Frankincense and Murder" (36)
"Handsel Monday" (36)
"Hard Lesson, The" (40)
"Hard Sell, The" (32)
Harm's Way (27)
"Hen Party, The" (40)
Henrietta Who? (12)
"Her Indoors" (32)
His Burial Too (17)

Hole in One (36)
"Home Is the Hunter" (32)
House Possessed, A (148)
House Without a Key, The (92)
House Without the Door, The (117)
I Met Murder on the Way (155)
Injury Time (31)
"In the Family Way" (41)
Johnny Under Ground (56)
Keeper of the Keys (106)
Knock at Midnight, The (154)
"Language of Flowers, The" (40)
"La Plume de ma Tante" (40)
Last Respects (26)
Last Writes (40)
Late Phoenix, A (16)
"Left, Right, Attention!" (40)
"Like to Die" (36)
Little Knell (34)
"Lord Peter's Touch" (31)
Losing Ground (37)
"Losing the Plot" (36)
"Managed Retreat, A" (41)
"Man Who Rowed for the Shore, The" (31)
Many Deadly Returns (64)
"Memory Corner" (31)
"Misjudgement of Paris, The" (32)
Miss Fenny (139)
Monkey on a Chain (153)
Most Contagious Game, A (11)
Mr. Christopoulos (151)
Murder a la Mode (51)
Murder Fantastical (59)
Murders in Volume 2 (115)
Night Ferry to Death (81)
Night Walk (129)
Nothing Can Rescue Me (119)
"One Under the Eight" (32)
"Operation Virtual Reality" (41)

Parting Breath (21)
Passing Strange (24)
Past Tense (38)
"Plane Fare" (40)
"Preyed in Aid" (36)
"Queen of Hearts, The" (40)
"Quick on the Draw" (40)
Religious Body, The (8)
Season of Snows and Sins (65)
Seven Keys to Baldpate (87)
Shadow of Murder, The (143)
Shirt Front, The (155)
Six-Letter Word for Death, A (82)
"Sleeping Dogs, Lying" (40)
Slight Mourning (19)
"Slight of Hand" (32)
"Soldier of the Queen, A" (36)
Some Die Eloquent (23)
Somewhere in the House (126)
"Spite and Malice" (41)
"Stars in Their Courses, The" (41)
Stately Home Murder, The (14)
"Steady as She Goes" (31)
Stiff News (33)
Sunken Sailor, The (46)
"These for Remembrance" (41)
"Time, Gentlemen, Please" (36)
To Kill a Coconut (72)
"Touch Not the Cat" (36)
"Trouble and Strife, The" (36)
Twice in a Blue Moon (84)
Unexpected Night (109)
When the Sun Goes Down (153)
Who Is Simon Warwick? (74)
Who Saw Her Die? (64)
"Widow's Might, The" (36)
"Wild Card, The" (36)
Witches' Sabbath (145)
Woman in the Woods, The (139)

Wrong Way Down, The (127)

www.ingramcontent.com/pod-product-compliance
Lightning Source LLC
Chambersburg PA
CBHW061654040426
42446CB00010B/1739